Bliss in the Wild

The Intentional Woman's Guide to Creating Everyday Joy

Written by Cyndi Swall

Illustrations by Leanne Rachel Allen

Bliss in The Wild. Copyright @ 2020 Cyndi A. Swall. All rights reserved.

Cyndiswall.com

ISBN: 9798617783065

Edited by Kristin McTiernan and Rachel Ellyn

Cover photography and design by Heather McKenzie

Illustrations and cover art by Leanne Rachel Allen

The scanning, uploading or distribution of this book via the internet or any other means without the permission of the author/publisher is illegal and punishable by law. The publication may not be reproduced, stored in a retrieval system or transmitted in whole or in part, in any form or by any means, electronic, mechanical, photocopying, recording or otherwise without the prior written permission of the author/publisher.
Cyndi A. Swall, Mission, KS 66202.
Please purchase only authorized editions, and do not participate in or encourage piracy of copyrighted materials. Your support of the author's rights is appreciated.

DISCLAIMER: The advice, suggestions and guidance contained within this book are based solely on the opinions and viewpoints of the author/publisher and are not all based on scientific studies, statistical analysis or similar sources. The author/publisher does not warrant the performance, effectiveness, applicability or outcomes of any of the advice, suggestions or guidance contained in this book.
The author and publisher disclaim any warranties (express or implied), merchantability or fitness for any particular purpose. The author/publisher shall in no event be held liable to any party for any direct, indirect, punitive, special, incidental or other consequential damages arising directly or indirectly from any use of this material, which is provided "as is" and without warranties of any nature or type.

Acknowledgments

Thank you to the following individuals who without their contributions and support this book would not have been published:

Kristen for her thoughtful and expedient editing.

Heather and Jodi for being my guinea pigs and giving priceless feedback. And to Heather for the beautiful cover design.

Scott for believing in me and brainstorming with me and generally being my cheerleader.

Leanne for her incredible talent and heartfelt illustrations.

Rachel for being my authoring mentor, publishing genius and holding the artistic fire to my ass.

This book is dedicated to
my freaking amazing daughter, Mariah
and to every woman who's tired
of waiting around
for something or someone else
to bring them happiness.

NOW is the time and YOU are the one.

Table of Contents

Introduction

Chapter 1: Redefining "Bliss"

Chapter 2: Why You Care

Chapter 3: Your Old Story

Chapter 4: Stop Tolerating

Chapter 5: Simplification

Chapter 6: Forgiveness

Chapter 7: Synchronicity

Chapter 8: Expectancy

Chapter 9: Connection

Chapter 10: Play

Chapter 11: Rituals

Chapter 12: Self-Lovin'

Chapter 13: Contentment

Chapter 14: Gratitude Through the Chaos

Chapter 15: Your New Story

Chapter 16: Everything Is a Miracle-or Nothing Is

Introduction

So, what's this bliss thing we keep hearing about and why is everyone following it? Two years ago, I couldn't have answered that question. In fact, I viewed it as somewhat of a myth, something to be categorized alongside unicorns and delicious fat-free salad dressing. Then one day, quite unexpectedly, bliss began to follow *me*.

I was having breakfast with a dear friend at our favorite pseudo-trendy bistro, feeling especially cosmopolitan. Enjoying our Eggs Benedict and the privacy of our conversation, the hostess proceeded to seat a boisterous teenage couple at the table approximately six inches to the left of us. In fact, they were so close, the young girl put her purse on top of mine because there was no more space. As I fought the irritation that began to sweep over me, I looked up and read her dusty brown graphic t-shirt. In pink letters, it said, "Follow Your Bliss." Suddenly, with no good explanation, this intrusion somehow seemed all right with me and I said to my friend, "I love the word bliss. Not sure exactly what it means, but it just feels like happy." We continued our meal without another mention.

Since we were in the heart of a beautiful shopping district, after breakfast, my friend and I wandered and chatted and window-shopped. We found ourselves in the Lucky Brand store where my petite, childless, executive friend, with lots of expendable income and a 28-inch waist, wanted to try on $300 jeans. While I waited, I picked up a rubber phone case from the counter to play with. On the back, it had a lotus flower inscribed with the word "bliss" below it. I thought how odd it was to see and acknowledge that word twice in an hour. I just smiled and put it back.

On my drive home, hours of shopping had me parched. I stepped into Latte Land for a pomegranate iced tea for the road. Cruising along, singing loudly to my favorite Kenny Loggins medley, my vocal chords needed a little refresh. As I brought the glass of tea to my lips, I couldn't believe what I was seeing. Printed on the side of my clear plastic cup was the word "bliss!" Okay, what is up with that? This was getting borderline creepy.

Meanwhile, in an alternate reality, I had started the process of writing a coaching book but struggled to settle on a single concept. So, given the events of the day, I wondered if this was a message related to my book. So, I decided to negotiate with God (you know what I'm talking about). I was raised in Missouri. It's the "Show Me" state. So, I said, "Here's the deal, God (we're tight). If I'm supposed to incorporate this bliss concept into my book, I need to randomly see the word one more time before I go to bed tonight."

Hours later, I was cooking dinner and my daughter was watching TV in the living room. When a commercial came on, I walked in to announce that dinner was almost ready. As I entered the room, I was drawn to a vision on the screen of rich, dark chocolate pouring the entire width of the monitor. The commercial was announcing Dove's sinful new bite-size truffles that they have so appropriately named…you guessed it—Bliss! I had to sit down. Now, not only was I sure of my mission, but it was available in three decadent flavors of chocolate confection. It was a perfect moment. Suddenly my vision was infinitely clear…discovering and cultivating happiness and helping others do the same. I'm not sure why this surprised me. I left my corporate executive coaching job when I realized I was much less interested in making people better leaders than I was in making my leaders happier people. My real work needed a more holistic approach.

Since then, not only have I blogged mostly about bliss, it has organically become the focus of my work at every level. To my clients, I am affectionately known as the Bliss Mentor and I travel the world showing people how to get bliss to follow *them*!

I promise this isn't a book that just blows glitter up your skirt about how every moment of your life can be filled with happiness and light. A world without contrast would be super lame and equally boring. My purpose here is to share with you some of the ways in which I've overcome destructive thought patterns and attracted more awesome into my own experience. I'm also gifting to you the best practices of my coaching clients who are making good stuff happen for themselves and others every day. Each moment you have a choice. And the choices you make determine your actions. Then your actions become your life. So, if you aren't waking up excited for the adventures of this new day, you have to ask yourself - What am I choosing?

MY BLISS MANIFESTO

Through connection, renewal, creativity & love, I inspire myself & others to live more meaningful, magical lives
filled with passion & possibility, so that we all may embody the transformative power of abundant happiness!

Chapter 1
Redefining Bliss

Life was never meant to be an all-or-nothing battle between misery and bliss. When a day's not perfect, it's not a failure.
It's just another day on the journey.
– Joseph Campbell, Originator of the Hero's Journey

So, in our on-going competition to keep up with the feminine ideal, there are countless daily opportunities for us to miss the bar set by Victoria's Secret, Martha Stewart, PTA room mothers, and Cosmopolitan magazine. One thing I've learned in working with hundreds of coaching clients over the years is the distinct need to expand our core definition of "bliss."

I've learned that naturally happy people don't live in a constant state of Zen. People who show up from a place of consistent joy are awake to the *whole* human experience—the good, the bad, and the ugly. Maybe that's not what you wanted to hear. Perhaps you had hoped this was a guidebook for being happy all the time. Try not to be disappointed. I'm not here to just help you find your happy place. I'm here to challenge your thinking about the concept of both bliss and chaos in your life.

What Do You Wear to a Pity Party?

I got a note on Facebook from someone one day that said, "I sense that something is wrong, yet your life is perfect. How could that be?"

Are you kidding me? I consider my life a blessing, don't get me wrong, but it's not for lack of the same crap everyone deals with. I'm a Bliss Mentor, not a Yogi. There's an important distinction I'd love to share with you. It's very possible for you to find happiness without achieving the pinnacle of spiritual and emotional utopia. Bliss doesn't mean you have your life all figured out and that problems elude you. (Spoiler Alert: That will never happen!) It just means you choose to find moments of appreciation and beauty, not just when the evidence is good, but through whatever monotony or hell is going on in your life.

Here's a little secret about me. A while back, I lost 75% of my income (too many eggs in one basket) and the man I loved (apparently not enough eggs in that basket) all in the same week! Let's just say that conditions were ripe for a pity party of extreme proportions. Now, I'd love to tell you that I just put on my big girl panties and brushed it off. Truth is, after a couple of weeks, I got tired of waking up with my eyes swollen shut from crying. This story has a happy ending, but I don't want to candy-coat it. I was beyond sad at the loss of my relationship. I had never felt more alone. And I was terrified at the reality of being "unemployed." I was raising a teenage girl by myself and I have always been my only source of income. Now I had no prospects in sight! I had slipped into a pretty dark place in my beliefs. Even for the most optimistic among us, I'm here to tell you it's okay to go there; in fact, it's important to go there. Just don't set up camp!

So, what do you wear to a pity party? For a while, you may wear sweats stained with Ben & Jerry's. But when you're ready, you trade in your Pebble's ponytail for a glimpse of sunlight. Stay grounded in the truth of who you are. **Remember this: naturally thin people don't eat diet food and inherently happy people possess an underlying belief, despite all evidence to the contrary, that everything is going to be okay.**
And it will be. Trust me.

Be Fully Present

Being able to become aware of your emotions and acknowledge them is the first step to healing. Here's the good news—you don't even have to be "healed" in order to experience bliss. It's not only possible, but essential, to be present in the fleeting moments of goodness in life while you are still mired waist-deep in misery and challenges. We'll talk more about that as we move through the bliss techniques in this book. For now, please know there is no emotional preparation or specific state of being that you need to acquire to be ready for what I'm going to share with you. I've heard it said that "Everybody seems normal until you get to know them." We all have our stuff that we're managing. Yes, shockingly, even I have baggage (but mine's cute and it matches)!

Seriously, I've learned true bliss can only come from experiencing ALL my feelings, not just the ones I'm proud of. I've also learned that just because something looks broken, doesn't mean it is. Be prepared! Once you set a new intention for your life and take action in that direction, the wheels are going to fall right off the bus of your current reality. You can't create a bigger life by living in your old circumstances. Some things and some people will get to go with you as you grow and evolve. But please know that some can't, or won't, and probably shouldn't.

Careful What You Ask For...

Have you ever been on a self-improvement power mission and somehow it seems like your life is getting worse? You know the drill: you've memorized the Kim Kardashian Butt Workout to the point that Icy Hot has become your signature scent. You religiously recite the affirmation cards you have taped to your bathroom mirror. You've showered your chakras, smudged your office, mastered Downward Dog and finally forgiven your fifth-grade teacher for making you spell "antidisestablish-mentarianism" in front of the class. You're seriously doing *all* the right things. So, what *is* the deal?

Bliss Tip: *Sometimes when your world appears to be falling apart, things are actually just falling away. Be willing to release the people, things, and circumstances that have kept you stuck in your old story.*

Anything that doesn't look like the new vision you have for your best life can't stay in your experience. That means the job you hate and the people who don't support you will be unconsciously seeking to move further away from you. That's textbook Law of Attraction stuff. Occasionally, true progress will exhibit itself as the end of a relationship or getting laid off. This is precisely why most people who desire a better life will never take the steps required to get there. Change, even for the better, is messy and generally disruptive. It's definitely not for the faint of heart. But those willing to feel the shift and move through the discomfort are the rare few who are now living the grandest expression of the vision they have for themselves.

Can You Say, "Paradigm Shift?"

Years ago, I began to see Zoloft and Prozac commercials on prime-time television, which told me that depression and anxiety had become so mainstream it was proving to be lucrative enough to advertise these medications to the general public. At the time, I was an Executive Coach on staff with a major telecom carrier. It was a great gig with killer benefits and all the swag I could fit into my Tumi roller bag. But after years of doing leadership coaching, I realized I was much less interested in just making people better leaders than I was in making my leaders *happier* people. And, truth be known, those who have good life balance, who are living in alignment with their values, and are investing in healthy relationships are not only instinctively better leaders, they're a helluva lot more fun to be around. Now, these are not people without challenges; they've just gotten really good at channeling their energy where they have some element of control.

Unique as Your Thumbprint

Bliss is a hot topic right now. Everybody's talking about it and no one really knows what it means. That's because every one of you has your own individual idea about what brings you contentment. The cool part is YOU get to define it and YOU can decide how much of it you are willing to allow into your experience.

Most people never find true bliss because they can't even articulate what it is they truly *want*. Dr. Michael Beckwith goes as far as to say that, as a species, we're suffering from what he calls an "Intention Deficit Disorder." I found this term both highly amusing and slightly sad. It's like embarking on a journey with no destination in mind. And unfortunately, this mentality has become our societal norm.

Cognitive research tells us that, barring any intervention on our part, the average human being in Western civilization takes in *nine* pieces of negative data every day for every *one* positive. What the...? I thought this was a staggering statistic and not one I particularly wanted to contribute to. Primarily, the "data" they refer to is a compilation of all the media we absorb, conversations with other people, and of course our own condescending self-talk. Is it any wonder most people have come to believe bliss is one of those luxuries afforded to other people, but probably not in the cards for them?

I'm not telling you this to bum you out. In fact, here's the really good news: We've all been graced in this life with super useful tools, things like free will and opposable thumbs and cognitive skills. These blessings allow us to do the important things in life, like the ability to text...and the power to make our own decisions about what goes into our head.

Garbage in - Garbage out

Your brain is basically a computer, right? So, we can choose to expose ourselves to more of the data that serves us and minimize the garbage we allow in. We do that by surrounding ourselves with positive people, proactively choosing our media, and telling a better story about who we are and what's possible for us.

Now this sounds simple enough, but we know it's not always easy. Hang with me here and, in the next few chapters, I'll see if I can't de-mystify things for you just a bit.

The premise of this book is twofold. A core expectation is you'll learn ways to attract *more* joy into your life….and you will. The lesser-known strategy is recognizing the awesomeness that already exists which you may be missing through the smokescreen of stress and interference that tends to cloud your perspective. That's not Pollyanna speak for "look for the silver lining in the eye of the freaking tornado." Just trust me on this one. Being open to the more stealth and subtle of life's little surprises yields infinitely more sustainable joy than the occasional "major life event."

The fact you're reading this book tells me you're more than ready for a quantum happiness leap. Before you embark on this bliss journey, I'm going to suggest you grab a small "Joy Journal" for your reflection. There will be several points throughout the book where I will ask you to take a BLISS BREAK and write your thoughts down. So, my advice to you now is just to relax, be open, strap in, and enjoy the ride!

Chapter 2
Why You Care

When a woman's mind, body, and spirit unite, miracles happen, her transformation becomes the gift that keeps on giving.
– Dr. Pamela Peeke, former Health Advisor to the Surgeon General

I can talk to anyone for ten minutes about what's going on in their life right now and tell you exactly what they've been focusing on and talking about for the past year or two. While I'd love to tell you that it's my highly developed Spidey coaching senses, the truth is, it's usually just a good old-fashioned case of self-fulfilling prophecy. **What you think about expands – period.** I'm not talking woo-woo stuff here. This has been scientifically proven time and time again.

Pick Your Study

A key area of focus for the Institute of HeartMath Research Center is exploring our emotions and how they affect our physiology. HMI's scientists, for years, have probed and proven the electrophysiology of intuition, our unconscious thoughts and how all things are unquestionably interconnected.

Back in the 80s, the U.S. Olympic team hired Dr. Denis Waitley to teach athletes the power of *Visual Motor Rehearsal.* Here are the observations from Dr. Waitley:

Using this program, Olympic athletes ran their event – but only in their mind. They visualized how they looked and felt when they were actually participating in their event.

The athletes were then hooked up to a sophisticated biofeedback machine, and its results told the real story about the value of visualization. The neural transmitters that fired were the same that actually fired the muscles in the same sequence as when they were actually running on the track!

This proved that the mind can't tell the difference between whether you're really doing something or whether it's just a visual practice. Dr. Waitley says, 'If you've been there in the mind, you'll go there in the body.'

Dr. Martin Seligman's fifty years of research at the University of Pennsylvania around Positive Psychology also reinforces this theory.

Even ancient scripture alludes to this: *For as a man thinketh in his heart, so is he.* (Proverbs 23:7).

This isn't a new concept. We all get it in theory. So, why is it so elusive in practice?

<u>You Break It – You Own It</u>

A friend of mine is a blues singer and he had the opportunity to play awhile at our favorite vegan restaurant while we were in New Hampshire one summer. As I was sitting there listening to him play, pondering the irony of singing the blues at the "Good Karma Café," I recognized how relevant the analogy was to our daily lives. It reminded me that the story we continue to tell about who we are and what's in the cards for us always dictates our experience – no matter where we are. We could be sitting in the midst of the most magical moment and completely not see it through the filter of our old beliefs or the clutter of our hectic thinking.

This was an empowering moment when I realized that **the world cannot give you joy and the world cannot take your joy away.** You own your own happiness. How cool is that? But with that awareness comes a certain amount of responsibility.

Bliss Tip: Anything high performance is high maintenance. There is truth to the old adage that "you get what you put into it." That applies to relationships, your health, your home, your work, even your emotional wellbeing. You must invest DAILY into what brings you happiness.

<u>The Care and Feeding of Your New Joy</u>

Like anything you want to grow, you have to nurture it, feed it, appreciate it, and most importantly, make it a daily practice. What is this *IT* that I keep referring to? This is the fun part where *you* get to decide what *IT* is. Do you even know what brings you joy? The first step toward awakening to bliss is recognizing it when you trip over it.

BLISS BREAK:
Before you go any further, I want you to grab your journal (get a head start on the next page). Put this as your header: <u>Cyndi's Joy List</u> (only, you know, use *your* name). Then number 1-100. Yes, I said 100. That wasn't a typo. I want you to make a list of 100 things that bring you joy and you can't stop until it's full. The first 30 or so are pretty easy. But once you get past your kids, your new convertible, Santa Margherita Pinot Grigio, stretch denim, and winning at Bunko, you may have to reach a little.

If you're at a stalemate on your list, I want you to dig a little deeper. This will require you to be fully present in the moment at several points throughout the day. Survey your surroundings. It may take you a day or two to complete your list and that's okay. Because there's a real likelihood the things you really love aren't in your environment right now. When was the last time you took an inventory of the things that bring you joy and made an effort to include those things in your daily life?

- Do you love the smell of pumpkin in the Fall?
- That yellow house on the corner by your daycare?
- A decaf, two-pump vanilla soy latte with extra foam?
- Singing Cyndi Lauper really loud in your car? (Maybe only me)

Think outside your beta fish tank and memories of joy will begin to return to you a little at a time. Include things you used to love but haven't factored into your life for a while.

- Did you used to love to salsa dance?
- Or grab a cherry Slurpee after school?
- Or read to your kids years ago?

Fair warning, though: you might just open the happiness floodgates if it's been a while since you've focused on YOU!

_____'s JOY LIST

1.
2.
3.
4.
5.
6.
7.
8.
9.
10.
11.
12.
13.
14.
15.
16.
17.
18.
19.
20.
21.
22.
23.
24.
25.
26.
27.
28.
29.
30.

Bliss Tip: To assist in making your Joy List, I want you to include ALL six of your senses! (Taste, Smell, Sound, Sight, Touch...and don't forget Feelings and Activities).

So, what's the point of creating this list other than to prove to yourself you can? Actually, that's a pretty valid reason alone, since 75% of my female clients can't do it on their first attempt. Why is it that, as women, we are so in tune with the needs of everyone around us, but many of us struggle to identify what *we* love most in the world? This list forces you to become aware of where you are and what you're feeling in the moment; you will also use it as a springboard for creating more INTENTIONAL joy in your world every day. Review your list each morning and commit to incorporating one thing into your experience each day. It could be something small like buying a lavender candle for your bath, getting a pedicure in the colors of your alma mater, or calling your friend from college who always makes you laugh so hard coffee spews out your nose. Maybe you'll boil yourself some shrimp, even though no one else in the house likes it, or buy something that makes you feel sexy and seduce your husband when he just comes in from the garage for a beverage. So much joy...so little time! Be creative!

The Point of Power

I'm going to show you a model that has been massively impactful in my life. I didn't create it, but I have my own take on how I use it. Every good coach taps into other great coaches and ideas. This one is credited to Meadow Devor. She is predominantly a money coach but has given me clarity on a number of topics. The following graphic describes the continuous cycle of manifesting in your life. What we know for sure is that everything ever been created began with a thought. But what follows may surprise you.

If I were to ask you where tangible creation begins to happen in this cycle, most of you would say *Actions*. In reality, your action is simply a symptom of what you are feeling. If you felt sad, you'd take one action. If you were optimistic, you'd take a different action. The point of power is actually in your *Feelings*. Thoughts and words are important to formulating your beliefs, but it's your emotions that incite the energy shifts needed for creation to take place.

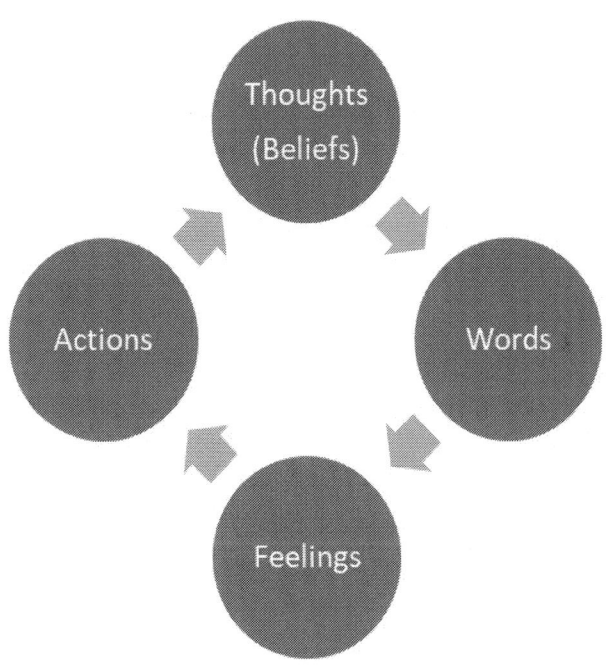

How Does That Make You Feel?

Let me give you an example most of us can relate to at some point in our lives. When I was working for the telecom company, they had a history of doing mass employee layoffs about once a year. As a leadership coach, I spent a lot of time talking people off the ledge during these events. So, let's assume the above cycle starts with a thought. If you have a belief (which is just a thought you think over and over again) that this layoff is a terrible thing, then you will speak about it with others in the same way. "The economy is bad. The package is unfair. Jobs are scarce. I'm too old or young or unskilled, don't have a degree..." If those are the things you are saying to yourself and anyone else who will listen, how do you think you're *feeling* about it? Probably scared, maybe angry, discouraged, or even hopeless. So, if that's how you're feeling, what kind of actions you are you likely to take? See how we propagate the cycle? And we do it in every area of our lives. The cycle is powerful and it's active with every thought, whether you're aware of it or not.

- What do you think and say about your body?
- What do you commiserate about with others every day?
- What thoughts and words bring up the strongest emotions in you?

Start paying very close attention to your language because you're writing your life story. More importantly, be in touch with how you are *feeling* in those moments, because how you're feeling is actively creating your future!

In the documentary, *The Secret*, Lisa Nichols refers to this as your "Emotional Guidance System." In simplest terms, whatever you chose to FEEL in each moment will attract to you more reasons to feel that way. Emotions are just indicators as to whether your thoughts are in alignment with moving you toward your desires or further away.
You become a magnet for all things aligned with that feeling.

Bliss Tip: Use your emotions to guide your thinking, not the other way around. The happiness of your life depends on the quality of your thoughts and your feelings will tell you if your thinking is creating what you want or more of what you don't want. If you are feeling lousy, then your thinking is damaging. You can know at every moment what kind of tomorrow you are creating by how you are feeling in this minute.

<u>Choose Again!</u>

You are NEVER at a choice-less moment. You are constantly deciding what you're going to eat and where you're going to turn and how you'll respond in any given situation. All of those decisions begin with a thought, spurred by a belief, so it's really all about thought. Those collective thoughts lead to feelings that drive our habitual actions and eventually become our lives. That's the deal! I'm not suggesting you monitor all of your thoughts. Since the average person thinks about sixty thousand thoughts a day, that's not only unrealistic, it's more than slightly neurotic.

Clients ask me all the time how to "quit" thinking a negative thought they have been harboring for a long time. Trying *not* to think about something is a fruitless task. It's like, "Don't think about pink elephants." Now what are you thinking about? The only way to quit thinking a counter-productive thought is to replace it with another thought. That's why many people use affirmations and vision boards to redirect their focus. Those are replacement techniques. We'll address this more in a later chapter.

What I hope to convey throughout this book is that a regular diet of blissful moments is not only possible, it's our natural state. Stress and angst come purely from resisting what is instinctive. A few small changes and daily practices with change your life in quantum ways! But first you must be willing to let go of the fables you have been repeating about your life that no longer serve you.

Chapter 3
Your Old Story

There is no greater agony than bearing an untold story inside you.
– Maya Angelou, Poet and Civil Rights Activist

We were all born with the inherent awareness we are hard-wired to do great things! You knew that when you came here. Yet, somewhere along the line, we are exposed to pieces of data — other people's opinions and media hype — that begin to distort our perception and impact our beliefs about what's achievable for us. Some of the most damaging and inaccurate beliefs we have about ourselves came from our childhood, usually from people who had our love and trust — our parents, teachers, older siblings, maybe even the church. Sometimes with the best of intentions, we are given "advice" and observations that are really just reflections of the other person's fears and flawed beliefs. But we take it all in and begin telling those stories ourselves as if they were fact. After you tell a story long enough, you start to embrace it and totally believe it.

Take an Inventory

Here's the good news: **Now that we're grown-ups, with no one else directing our conscious thinking, it's time to enter the reflection stage where we get to re-imagine our lives the way** *we* **want it to look.** But first, you have to get real about what your habitual thoughts have been and what you've been experiencing of late. Here, I'm going to ask you to BRIEFLY take a *non-judgmental* inventory of your current manifestations (meaning, what's happening in your life right now). How do they differ from what you'd like your world to look like? There's the gap.

Just Missed the Mark

The first time I walked into a "new thought" church, I was 11 years old. My parents had four children, so up to that point, they pretty much put us on whatever vacation bible school bus came by our house just to catch a break! But it was by no coincidence when we wandered into this place. A gentleman by the name of Rocco Errico was speaking. It was to be a day that would change my life forever. Rocco is a biblical scholar who also happens to be proficient in Aramaic and Hebrew exegesis. He was explaining how the original bible was written in Aramaic and how it doesn't translate literally into English. He also described how words meant different things 2,000 years ago…like the word "sin" was an archery term that simply meant "to miss the mark." Even in my pre-adolescent mind, I remember feeling enormous relief. For me, this was a message of hope and I was excited about the possibility I wasn't doomed to pay eternally for my uneducated mistakes—that I had some control over the outcome of my life. It meant to me that my fumbling growing pains and missteps were part of the evolution that I would come to call my learning experience. Whew! Most importantly, it meant when I screwed up, I got to choose again.

What this means to you is, whatever story you have been telling yourself and the world about who you are is most likely not even entirely your story. It's a culmination of other people's stories that you just never questioned for validity. Keep in mind not all of your story is inaccurate. A lot of the things you currently say to yourself are true for you and support your growth. The road to bliss doesn't require a total shift in lifestyle or consciousness. But it is time to separate fact from fable if you want to break out of the loop of negativity that is keeping you stuck in your "stuff."

So, what is *your* stuff? Your stuff is the collective conversation you keep having with yourself about who you are and what you're capable of. I want you to think about your self-talk on any given subject. Not your belief about the subject, but the *words* you use when you talk to yourself.

Your old (current) story may sound something like this:

- "No one wants to hire someone my age."
- "I could never wear that. I'm too fat (short/tall/old/frumpy)."
- "I'm destined to live from paycheck to paycheck. My industry just doesn't pay well."
- "I'll never find time for myself until my kids are grown and gone."
- "I'm not smart enough."
- "Why would someone pay me to do this?"
- "I'm so stressed out. I can't take this pressure."
- "I can't do anything right!"
- "How could I be so stupid?"
- "No one here likes me."
- "The economy is terrible. I'll never sell my house/get my business off the ground."
- "I'll be okay once I _____ (fill in the blank: lose 20 lbs., finish my degree, meet Prince Charming, etc.)."

Bliss Tip: Be careful how you talk to yourself because YOU are listening!

Let's be honest here—would you ever let anyone talk to you the way you talk to yourself?! *Seriously?* I think not. That's your old story. As Dr. Phil would ask us, "How's that workin' for ya?"

Oftentimes, we are our own worst enemy when it comes to the happiness paradigm. To quote my favorite Marianne Williamson passage, *"Our deepest fear is not that we are inadequate. Our deepest fear is that we are powerful beyond measure. It is our Light, not our Darkness, that most frightens us. We ask ourselves, 'Who am I to be brilliant, gorgeous, talented, fabulous?' Actually, who are you not to be?"*

As a coach, I have worked with women from homeless shelters and I have coached women who are CEOs of Fortune 500 companies, and I find there's one common theme that emerges with every woman I've ever worked with, regardless of their level of success: it's the irrational and innate belief that we are somehow inherently broken in some way. The idea that if you could fix that one thing (whatever yours is), then you'd be all right. Then you'd feel successful, or lovable, or worthy. I'm here to reassure you, not only are you *not* broken, you're not alone.

<u>It's on the Internet—It Must Be True</u>

The real challenge with saying these things over and over again is the more you say them, the more truth they carry. Psychologists have a term for that. It's called "confirmation bias" and it simply means we seek out evidence to support what we already believe to be true. If you ever question the theory, all you have to do is go on Facebook during a political election. There is evidence to support literally whatever you believe in. If you believe people don't like you, then you'll be hyper-alert for examples of where that might show up. You'll begin to make up motives for other people's behavior and eventually become mega paranoid. If you believe you're too old to be a desirable candidate for a job, you'll assume every rejection letter is because of age and it will begin to inhibit the actions you take (remember the manifesting cycle). When you find yourself thinking thoughts like these, it just means you've "missed the mark" and you get to choose again.

Put on your Big Girl Panties

I remember when I was in high school. I was on the hunt for a homecoming dress and I was struggling to find something that would fit. I was 5'8" and 15 lbs. I was not remotely fat but I was "curvy." I had boobs and hips. Granted, now that we put so many steroids in our food, most 12-year-olds are built like that, but that wasn't the case when I was young. All my friends were built like pipe cleaners and all the cute dresses were shaped like that, too. If I could find one to fit my ta-tas, it hung like a potato sack. If it fit everywhere else, I couldn't squeeze my butt into it. I recall sitting on the floor of the dressing room sobbing. My mother, in her infinite good intentions, put her hand on my shoulder and said, "Honey, don't worry about it. You're just a big girl."

Okay, during the teenage phase of body insecurities, I don't have to tell you how that might be interpreted by a 16-year-old girl? Truth was, I *wasn't* a big girl. I was a tall girl and I was built like a woman. But I internalized this comment completely and, as a result, lived most of my adult life about 20 lbs. overweight, just slightly bigger than my healthiest weight. I made this message a part of my story and it impacted everything from what I wore to where I went and who I would let get close to me. It was probably the fifty-year lesson before I finally figured out that it wasn't my story at all and I could tell whatever story I wanted about my body.

BLISS BREAK:
On the next few pages, you're going to be writing down the things you say to yourself on a regular basis that don't support you. Everyone has their own patterns of self-talk. Some things you say to yourself make you feel encouraged and brave and capable. But if you are encased in a human body, there's a very high likelihood you have some things you say to yourself that make you feel less than stellar. It's important to identify those thoughts and words because they are shaping your reality.

This is not a list of BELIEFS, but rather a peek into your personal DIALOG. Consider the areas of your life where you tend to tell the most damaging stories. Using the examples listed for prompts, write out the things you SAY TO YOURSELF in each of these key areas...

BODY/ WELL-BEING
Example:
All the women in my family have big thighs. I'm destined to inherit them.
OR
I've been sickly since I was a child. It's just my lot in life.

_____
_____
_____
_____
_____
_____
_____
_____

FINANCES/CAREER
Example:
I'll never be able to catch up. I can't get a break.
OR
There's no way I can ever get promoted without a degree.

_____
_____
_____
_____
_____
_____
_____
_____

RELATIONSHIPS
Example:
The odds of meeting someone special at my age are slim to none.
OR
Why would anyone want to be friends with me?

_____
_____
_____
_____
_____
_____
_____
_____

CAPABILITIES
Example:
I'll never get this figured out. I'm too stupid.
OR
You can't teach an old dog new tricks.

_____
_____
_____
_____
_____
_____
_____
_____

NOTE: Don't let this activity bum you out. These are just data points. You can and will shift this story. I'm proud of you for being so straight-up honest with yourself. I promise we're going to revisit this list later in the book and start replacing this limiting language with a more empowering narrative.

There is a small catch:
For every story you tell, there is a tangible and measurable payoff.

You are getting something from your story, and you have to be prepared to release the need for the pay-off before you can let go of your story. Maybe the payoff is sympathy, or empathy, or maybe even financial. Perhaps elements of your story provide you with an excuse not to have to do something you don't want to do. It's even possible your story keeps you tied to someone you are afraid of losing, even though they're not good for you, whether it be a romantic partner, business associate, family, or an alleged friend.

I want you to challenge your thinking about your own story. Take the time to recognize how you talk to yourself and whether that kind of relationship is one you care to continue. Make the commitment to yourself right now to allow only loving, supportive people into your life. And maybe you can start with the amazing Chica in the mirror? Just sayin'.

Chapter 4
Stop Tolerating

You teach people how to treat you by what you allow, what you stop, and what you reinforce. What are you tolerating?
– Tony A. Gaskins, Jr., Motivational Speaker and Life Coach

Simply put – you are completely defined by what you tolerate. And allowing toxic tolerations to persist in your experience will suck the life right out of you. So, why do you think we accept so many circumstances that are less than what we deserve or need? From a very early age, you may have been taught not to complain or moan about stuff, but to accept what is put in front of you and be happy to have it! There is still some perceived virtue in being the martyr, in making sure everyone else has their needs met first. Though a gross generalization, that's historically a woman thing and I'm here to remind you it's a very outdated model. You can find great joy in being a caregiver without sacrificing yourself in the process. I love doing thoughtful things for other people. That's actually on my Joy List. Additionally, I've learned to care enough about myself and my relationships now to ask for what I need too.

It's the Mosquitoes

I wouldn't be a very good coach if I just gave you more stuff to *do*. That would be the opposite of bliss. So, in order to free up energy for creating what you want more of in your life, you have to become aware of what is consuming so much of your energy and efforts right now. No doubt, you can name your major stressors, the big-ticket issues that consume your thoughts, but you may be surprised to hear those aren't the primary culprits for energy leaks.

It's the almost invisible, day-to-day annoyances that culminate into the life-sucking vitality drains which do the most damage. It's the tolerations that sneak up on us so stealthily over time that we don't notice until they've become a part of our daily lives. Hang tight. In a minute, we'll address the key areas of your life where these are most likely to show up, causing you undue stress.

Bliss Tip: If you're watching CNN or Zombie Apocalypse before you go to bed at night, STOP that! New cognitive research shows whatever you are thinking about the last five minutes before you enter REM sleep, your subconscious will gestate on **all night long**! That's why you wake up with that inexplicable feeling of doom when nothing is really wrong. Use that five minutes to wind down rather than gear up. Do some Creative Visualization or write in your Gratitude Journal - Let your subconscious work for you rather than against you.

Not to Be Confused with Tolerance

Let me just clarify for those of you who might be thinking I'm suggesting you become a less tolerant person. I don't mean that at all.

TOLERATING ≠ TOLERANCE

Webster's dictionary defines *Tolerance* as: being accepting of views, beliefs, practices, etc. of others that differ from one's own; freedom from bigotry or prejudice.
Tolerating means: to refrain from interfering with or prohibiting something undesirable or unpleasant, even if you disagree or it may cause personal harm.

Clearly, there's a distinguishable difference in impact between being annoyed by your friends' opposing political posts on social media and allowing others to seriously take advantage of you or not addressing your own destructive habits.

In his book, *Unlock Your Personal Potential,* Richard Bisiker lists three areas where we tend to tolerate unwanted circumstances the most:

1. In the behavior of **Others**
2. In our **Own B**ehavior
3. In our **Environment**

What We Tolerate from Others

This is a no-brainer because we tend to suspect that most all of our stress is driven by the antics of others anyway. While that may not be entirely accurate, we can't ignore the magnitude of these outside influences. What we tolerate from others varies largely in personal impact. You may be tolerating something as minor as an occasional noisy neighbor or as destructive as consistent physical or verbal abuse. Whatever the violation, our happiness—and sometimes our survival—depends upon our ability to recognize these daily disturbances and draw a new line in the sand. What's really okay with you and what's totally *not* okay? You need to be able to answer that question with certainty and more importantly, take action to eliminate these bliss-busters. I don't mean, "It bugs me when you slurp your soup." A real toleration is defined as the stuff others do that has an acute or long-term negative impact on your health or happiness. In a bit, I'm going to offer you the opportunity to identify the tolerations in your own life.

Some examples for OTHERS may include:

- Not picking up after themselves
- Talking down to you
- Being financially indebted to you
- Chronically late
- Not meeting their commitments
- Lying
- Dishonesty
- Anything that diminishes how you feel about yourself or the relationship

What We Tolerate from Ourselves

Would you ever let anyone talk to you the way you talk to yourself? Of course not! And you certainly wouldn't talk to anyone else that way. So, what's the deal? The place that women have served in history is partly responsible for our propensity towards making sure everyone else's needs are met before ours. But we're all grown up now and considerably evolved as a gender. We can make choices that weren't available to our moms and grandmothers. We can bring home the bacon, fry it up in a pan, or choose not to. And that's cool too. You're probably already keenly aware of your own habits, especially the ones that aren't serving you so much. We tend to be hyper-alert to our own shortfalls. This list will be the easiest one to complete because these are the judgments you are running through your head all the time. That said, there are likely some blind spots here for you as well. Take a look at some of the tolerations showing up in your "Others" and "Environment" category and ask yourself if there may be something you're doing (or not doing) to influence any of those too.

Some examples for YOURSELF may include:

- Procrastination
- Not eating right or exercising your body
- Negative self-talk
- Working all the time (no play)
- Judgment (of self and others)
- Settling for less than you deserve (people, places, and things)
- Complaining
- Anything that diminishes your self-esteem or keeps you from living the life of your dreams

What We Tolerate in Our Environment

Environment includes *any* place you go throughout your day on a regular basis. I'm talking about your home, your vehicle (or lack of either), school, workplace, corner pub, common shopping locales, friends' homes, or kids' events. You may have to carry a little notebook with you throughout your day to identify how many of these environmental factors really come into play for you. We become so accustomed to all our tolerations that they become our norm and we may not even notice them anymore. We've just learned to unconsciously adapt to them and they become part of the "story" we tell about our life.

When I bought my first house, it was an older home that had these beautiful vintage glass doorknobs. I loved them. I didn't want to replace them, but I had a challenge with the one on the front door. If you didn't push in on the knob just right as you turned it, it would literally come off in your hand! And, of course, it always happened when I was in the biggest hurry. It got to the point where, as I got within a few feet of the door, I could feel my blood pressure go up. Now, I did notice a tiny hole on the side of the knob which appeared to be the home of a teeny, lost antique screw that surely no one made any more (which was my story)…so I resigned myself to the fact I was just going to have to deal with it if I kept this knob. One day, I was reading a book on the sofa when someone unexpectedly rang the doorbell. I got up to answer it, still wearing my reading glasses. As I approached the knob, my new-found vision exposed that the tiny hole was actually six-sided. You homeowners know where I'm going with this. Yep, it was an Allen (hex) wrench, which I coincidentally had a whole set of in my junk drawer. I got out my wrench and tightened it up. It never came off again. For two years, I battled that damn doorknob! This is a great example of an environmental toleration which could have easily been eliminated and saved me a lot of grief.

Some examples for ENVIRONMENT may include:

- That mustard-colored kitchen you've been meaning to paint for years
- The front porch step with a chip out of it you just know someone is going to break an ankle on
- Clutter (You know who you are)
- Not enough space
- Old, outdated clothing
- Staying at the job that sucks the life out of you
- Poor lighting
- Weird smells
- Renting when you want to buy
- Living in a city or neighborhood that doesn't feel like home
- Any place or circumstance that depletes your personal comfort or makes you feel ill at ease

BLISS BREAK:
Give some thought to the behaviors and circumstances in your life, both big and small, that you have been tolerating for entirely too long. Make your own list in the following key areas and make an effort to eliminate these energy-busters one at a time. Use as much paper as you need – grab a legal pad! You will be amazed at how much time, effort and emotional energy is being spent on managing these irritations. Write with fervor – this feels REALLY good!

My Toleration List

Things I have been tolerating in other people's behavior...

_____

_____

_____

_____

_____

_____

_____

_____

_____

_____

_____

_____

My Toleration List

Things I have been tolerating in my own behavior...

_____

_____

_____

_____

_____

_____

_____

_____

_____

_____

_____

_____

My Toleration List

Things I have been tolerating in my environment...

_____

_____

_____

_____

_____

_____

_____

_____

_____

_____

So, if all we do is make the list, we're simply complaining…and that doesn't exactly foster bliss. Once you have completed your initial list, your challenge is to start finding ways to eliminate or minimize these tolerations one at a time. I say "initial" list because this is an on-going process. As time goes by, you will find that you've accumulated some new tolerations without realizing it. Make a fresh list every few months and celebrate your new freedoms.

Bliss Tip: *Truth Is: in most cases, ignorance isn't really bliss. Just being more aware that they exist is the first step towards freedom from them. Many tolerations are just habits that we've accepted as our lot in life without pausing to envision our day-to-day world sans these stressors.*

Time to release these energy drains! Scan your list and identify where you will start to clean the proverbial physical and emotional house. Pick a few easy ones off the list to get some early wins. Set good boundaries. Think a new thought. Freshen up your space. Love up on yourself a little every day.

Biggest Bang for Your Bliss Buck

While it's important to pinpoint the stuff we no longer want to experience, extended focus on what you *don't* want is the opposite of bliss and attracts more yucky feelings and experiences. For this reason, the remainder of the book has you putting your energy towards the actions, thoughts, and emotions that take you where you *do* want to hang out more often. Because happiness is a pretty nebulous term, you alone can decide what gets you there. Know this could change depending on your circumstances. Yet, in my many years as a women's transformational coach, I *have* identified some trends around what kinds of things tend to give most of us the biggest bang for our bliss buck.

I'd love to tell you that if you follow my magical three-step process, your life will be spontaneously filled with rainbows and unicorns and carrot cake with no calories in it. In reality, finding joy is a conscious choice, yet there are a number of practices that can guide you closer to experiencing your own daily dose of awesome (or contentment at the very least). The fact that you picked up this book tells me you're a ready and enthusiastic participant, so I'm excited to share some of these best practices with you!

Okay, in no particular order…here we go!

Chapter 5
Simplification

*The ability to simplify means to eliminate the unnecessary
so that the necessary may speak.*
– Hans Hofmann, Renown Artist and Teacher

Years ago, my (then) husband read a book that convinced him the Earth was going to shift on its axis and the only surviving population would be those residing in the middle of Idaho. He wanted us to sell all of our belongings, buy a trailer, and homestead there. (Seriously, you can't make this stuff up!) Now, I love Idaho, but if you look on a map, you'll realize that the middle of Idaho is totally uninhabited by most anything that walks on two legs, with the exception of maybe Grizzlies. And as much as I loved my husband, I had grown admittedly accustomed to the finer things in life: things like electricity and neighbors and Starbuck's decaf two-pump vanilla lattes (no whip, extra foam). Needless to say, he is now my ex-husband and think he lives happily somewhere in a cave with his dogs. I guess the term "simplify" is relative based on how complicated your life is right now. For the purpose of this discussion, I'm going to define simplify as "removing negative chaos." There are very effective ways to simplify that don't require quite that extreme lifestyle changes.

<u>Set Your Own Standards</u>

It's about taking 100% responsibility for your life and editing out those things that no longer serve you. You have to be able to separate the *nice to have* from the *need to have* when making decisions about the return on your energy investment.

I was raised by a mother who was clinically bi-polar before they knew exactly what that was or how to effectively treat it. On her manic days, she was wildly creative. We never just had birthday parties. We had major events with tents and catering and small circus elephants! (Okay…slight exaggeration, but you catch my drift). Mom shaped our pancakes into Disney animals and made fashion-forward Barbie clothes out of socks. As much fun as that was as a kid, when I grew up and got my own place, I was constantly in fear people were evaluating my entertainment savvy every time they entered my home. After all, I had big shoes to fill!

When my daughter was starting kindergarten, I thought it only appropriate I throw her a party in the backyard to celebrate her right-of-passage into big kid school. Of course, it was early August in the Midwest, which means 100 degrees in the shade with no breeze whatsoever. Very early the morning before her party, I stood alone on my private deck wearing nothing but a silk teddy, enjoying a cup of java and admiring my well-earned manicured lawn, when I suddenly realized I had missed a rogue weed in the back garden. Thinking my guests would surely notice my blatant foliage disregard, I wandered out in my jammies to pull those taunting rascals with my bare hands. With some success, I managed to pull them out left-handed without spilling a drop of cinnamon vanilla decaf. But there was one pesky strand of ivy that had wound itself around the copper base of a glass bird bath. After a failed one-handed attempt, I put my coffee down, cupped the glass bowl in my hands and tried to pull the bird bath out of the ground to free the weed. Brilliant in theory, only I hadn't anticipated the glass bowl would snap in half and shear my left index finger all the way to the bone. I'll spare you the graphics. It was icky and resulted in two surgeries and months of physical therapy. Suffice to say that I learned a significant lesson that weekend about knowing when to say "good enough."

I called my dear friend, Pam, to come the next morning to help me prepare for the party. Her voice sounded perplexed on the phone. "What were you doing again?" she asked. I relayed the details of my horrific bird bath incident. "I thought this was a kindergarten party?", she asked. Her response was nothing shy of life-altering. "Good God, Cyndi. Put some hot dogs on the grill and turn the sprinkler on. You don't have to make topiary out of your shrubs!" Wiser words have never been spoken. I get it now.

BLISS BREAK:
In your quest to get some elusive time back for the things you really long to do, consider some of the areas on the next page to help release some of the superfluous activities that may be eating away at your Google calendar. Recall how you feel while you are engaged in each activity and whether you are there with purpose or you just got roped in out of guilt or a sense of obligation.

Ways to Simplify Your Life

1. Tasks that are no longer necessary:
   _____
   _____
   _____

2. Things other people think I should do:
   _____
   _____
   _____

3. Philanthropic activities that I don't enjoy or don't utilize my strengths:
   _____
   _____
   _____

4. Professional organizations that take up too much time or offer minimal return:
   _____
   _____
   _____

5. Recreational affiliations I have because I feel obligated or has become a habit:
   _____
   _____
   _____

6. Financial or other goals that are ego-driven:
   _____
   _____
   _____

7. One-sided relationships and other people who drain my energy:
   _____
   _____
   _____

Nature Abhors a Vacuum

It's not so much what we add to our life that gives us peace of mind as it is what we are willing to let go of. Releasing outdated patterns of behavior frees up space in your life for what *really* matters. There are four key areas to consider when letting go of stuff:

> Relationships
> Habits/Thinking
> Physical Stuff
> Philanthropy

Relationships

This is always a tough one because most women don't like to think of people as disposable. Most of us will try everything within our power to salvage a relationship. While it's a loving practice to see the best in others, it's a healthy practice to know when a partnership has run its course. I'm not just talking about romance. Consider business associates you're not aligned with, family members that warrant a bit more distance, and peripheral 'friends' who suck the life out of you and bring very little to *your* life.

I'm reminded lately that sometimes you have to release people who have brought an enormous amount of joy into your life. Many of us Baby Boomers are saying goodbye to our parents. There's no way to prepare for that transition. But it is the circle of life and being able to lovingly release them to their next great adventure is paramount to emotional freedom.

My daughter, Mariah, is recently out of high school. Instead of starting college right away, she graduated and immediately left for a gap year program in Central America. It was going to be an amazing experience for her, but I've been a single mom since she was three and a half years old. We've grown up together and we're a team. On some days, she's such an adult and needs for nothing; other days, she'd have a bad day and will come over and crawl in bed with me. But now I was seeing more days of self-sufficiency than not. She researched this program, raised money, packed herself, updated her passport, and stepped onto the plane alone. I was thinking about how she really has made the transition to independence. My days of her needing me are limited. Then, less than an hour after they left, I got a text that said, "I miss you already Momma. I can't wait to come home." We're both learning to let go. I don't pretend this is easy. Be patient with yourself and allow space to grieve the changes. Then allow yourself to heal.

Bliss Tip: *Remember that people are in your life for a reason, a season, or a lifetime. As you tell a new story about your life, you set in motion the chain reaction that makes those dreams come true. And when you do, anyone who doesn't support your new vision doesn't get to play with you anymore. As you start creating the life you desire, you'll know who's up to making that journey with you and who isn't.*

Habits

In David Dow's book, *What I've Learned from Dying*, he suggests that every pattern of behavior starts with a mental or physical trigger which focuses our thoughts down a certain trajectory. He says that, if you can identify the trigger, you can change the behavior. For example, I set an intention to do my visioning and set my priorities for the day when I first woke up, before I got distracted by outside influences. Here was the rub. I was using my cell phone for an alarm clock. So, without thinking, I would pick up my phone, turn off the alarm, but having the phone in my hand triggered me to check my email and FB and Twitter. It was truly an automatic response based on having the device in my hand. So I bought a tabletop alarm clock and plugged my phone in across the room to disarm that trigger.

Let's say you're trying to lose weight and change your eating habits. But there's a Dunkin Donuts at the base of the elevator leading up to your office. You may not even be hungry, but the smell of baking pastries triggers an auto response, causing you to stop and grab a glazed every morning on your way in. If you can recognize the trigger, you can become awake to it and replace the behavior with something more affirming. If you know it's a trigger, you can take another route or pack yourself a yummy, healthier breakfast snack to look forward to.

Generally speaking, two things can't occupy the same space at the same time! Trying NOT to think about something is actually keeps it in your per view. The only way to stop a thought or a behavior is to replace it with another one.

Physical Stuff

I ran across a book the other day entitled, "Essentialism." The author talks about how, in most modernized civilizations, we over-value our stuff. We have learned to define ourselves by what we have, not who we are, which leads to a global sense of not-enough. We struggle to let go of tangible evidence of our success or remnants of memories we once shared.

Our houses are getting bigger and our families are getting smaller. The storage unit business has quadrupled in the last six years because people have run out of room in their homes for all their crap and it's spilling over into storage. I read a term in an airline magazine that I loved; this lifestyle was labeled "Stuffocation." The concept advocated trading in the chronic collecting of *things* for collecting of more *experiences*. Experiences make us more interesting people. Would you rather the person next to you tell you about their sofa or about their safari? The message isn't anti-stuff. It's anti *too much* stuff.

Don't get me wrong. I'm all about the creature comforts. I love beautiful things around me, but I am learning to edit out the things I don't absolutely love because they become interference which keeps me from enjoying my true treasures.

It's the Thought That Counts

Now that all the kids in the family are pretty much adults, the practice of holiday gift giving became nothing short of superfluous. We drew names and basically told the person what to buy us. Then we'd open the present we asked them to buy us and act surprised. So, last year, we opted to start a new tradition. We decided to scrap the gift exchange and spend the money on an experience together. Lots of great ideas were thrown out – everything from a cooking class at the Culinary Center to a tubing at a local ski resort. We landed on a holiday Murder Mystery party called "Ho Ho Homicide." It was unconventional and hilarious and one of my most memorable Christmases ever.

Kondo It! Does It Bring You Joy?

When I was a teenager, I never shopped for clothing alone. My mom always went with me and had very specific ideas about what I should buy. Now, understand my mom is a beautiful combination of French and Indian with brunette hair and brown eyes and she looks amazing in jewel tones. Her personality is bigger than life, so she was drawn to items with a flair for the dramatic. I have my Dad's alabaster skin, blond hair, and green eyes. When Mom wears red lipstick, she looks exotic. When I put it on, I look like an Irish hooker. I was thirty years old when I looked in my closet and realized there weren't ten things in there I would have bought of my own accord. So, I bagged up everything except a couple pair of jeans and a shirt or two and hauled it all to the Goodwill. It took me a while to rebuild a wardrobe, but it was very cathartic to release someone else's perception of who I was and begin to build my own.

Philanthropy

Finally, I can't address a group of women without bringing this up. Our gender has created a legacy of being in service to others. It's a part of who we are and what makes us thrive, both personally and collectively. But I'm starting to notice signs that busy is the new black. And if you're a giver by nature, I don't even have to tell you too much of a good thing is toxic. This is about understanding the difference between doing something you're *called to do* or doing it because *someone called you*. It's about releasing the need to be all things to all people.

Bliss Tip: *Here are some criteria to use when determining if something is yours to do. Only take on things that:*

- *You're deeply inspired by*
- *You're particularly talented at*
- *Meets a significant need in the world that you're passionate about*

It's about releasing the need to be perfect, either socially or professionally. One moment at a time, you have to lighten your load. Be honest with yourself about what wears you down and let those activities go. Evaluate what brings you joy (pull out your Joy List from Chapter 2) and do more of that. I encourage you to take the time to listen to your Emotional Guidance System. Ask what's yours to release now. Listen carefully and you can hear the sound of everything that doesn't matter disappear.

<u>Permission to Be Excused</u>

Do you ever wish someone could write you a pass to get you out of your responsibilities just for a day or two? Or better yet, a break from others' perceptions of your responsibilities? I'm reminded of an episode of *The Wonder Years* where the mom went on strike to inspire her slacking family to help out around the house. As the plot progresses, you realize it wasn't so much that she needed them to do more chores; she just wanted to be appreciated for her contribution. That struck a chord with me, but not because I don't feel appreciated. I totally do. But as a recovering over-functioner, the realization hit me. I was training people to count on me for things they were fully capable of doing themselves. But, why should they? I mean, really.

For whatever our *dysfunction* of choice is, there's a clear and tangible payoff here, also. For us "all things to all people" addicts, the reward comes in the form of appreciation. It's a powerful intoxication indeed. Appreciation is a form of love but can come with some significant strings attached. While it's nice to be loved for what you *do*, I am learning to see sweet value in just being loved for who I *am*. I invite you to check in with your crazy swamped self and see where you may be filling your schedule with other people's agendas at the expense of accomplishing your own objectives. Just because your Outlook is full doesn't mean you're doing anything. Maybe we over-commit to avoid our own stuff. Nothing ventured, nothing lost, right? And besides, someone else's life is an easy fix. We're too emotionally attached to ours. Way too messy!

I finally gave myself permission to take a couple of months away from planning and marketing to get super clear about how I'm spending my time…and for whom. I asked myself some tough questions about my personal mission and the activities I was letting distract me. If you're wondering what your own self-imposed interferences might be, take a look at your own calendar and you will clearly see the story unfold.

I want to be a good friend, an engaged parent, and a supportive partner. I want to be there for the people I care about when they need me. But my new vision is to love from a place of individual expansion. I'll choose pro bono work that is meaningful to me and release the need to be the "Official Prioritizer" for those I deem less productive.

Is it possible to just silently know that no one will ever do it as well as you could (that's a given), then allow the rest of the world to win, fail, and manage their own journey?

"What?!" …just breathe with me…

Perhaps it's time to trust that the rest of humankind has come here fully equipped with the same capacity to problem solve and take care of themselves as me. Unlikely as that seems, I'm willing to put my Wonder Woman outfit in the back of the closet and take my time back.

Raise your right hand and repeat after me:

"The most damaging things I can do for those I love are the things they can and should do for themselves. I release the need to function for everyone around me. They'll be fine. Today, I choose me."

Living your truth is asking yourself what is *really* important and then having the courage and wisdom to build your life around those answers, even at the risk of disappointing others. Are you ready to join me? Come on…I'll write you a note.

Chapter 6
Forgiveness

*As I walked out the door toward the gate that led to my freedom, I knew
if I didn't leave my bitterness and hatred behind,
I would still be in prison.*
– Nelson Mandala, former President of South Africa

I want to cover this one early, not just because of the impact it has on every aspect of your life, but also because this is the area where I tend to get the most resistance from my coaching clients. But hang in there with me. While you may be completely justified in the reasons behind your bitterness, what I know for sure is you can never achieve a state of bliss while simultaneously harboring resentment. They're mutually exclusive.

Anger acts like a toxin which flows through your life and contaminates every opportunity where joy could surface. It's always in the back of your thoughts and unconsciously makes you feel undeserving of your good, even if you have every right to be angry. You've heard it said forgiving another person doesn't condone the behavior. You're not saying it was okay for them to violate you in any way. Forgiveness is the gift you give to *yourself* to free you from the grief. You take your energy back and spend it on a much more worthy endeavor – your future happiness.

The Wisdom to Know the Difference

I'm always reminded of the Serenity Prayer when we talk about forgiveness:

*Grant me the Serenity to accept the things I cannot change,
Courage to change the things I can
and the Wisdom to know the difference.*

"…Wisdom to know the difference" is the operative phrase here. We spend most out of our lives and emotional energy lamenting about the behaviors of other people. We replay conversations in our heads and commiserate these betrayals to our friends to get further validation about our right to stay angry or hurt. We all do it. I recall my very close friend of over 20 years. Let's call her Janet. In our long and supportive tenure, we went through the deaths of three parents, the birth and rearing of my child, eight home moves and remodels, and years of joint vacations, countless heartbreaks and celebrations together. We were best friends, I thought for eternity. Then one day, she just quit returning my calls and wouldn't even open the door when I went to her house. It was beyond weird. If I had done something to upset her, I had no idea what it was.

On May 1st, after three weeks of not speaking to me, I stopped by a local nursery to pick up some flower seedlings. It was a May Day tradition we shared every year. We'd buy and plant our Spring blooms together at both of our houses. I shopped solo, set the pots on her front step with a card and pulled away. A couple of days later, I drove by and saw she had planted the flowers, but no word from here. That was over ten years ago. To this day, we are estranged with no explanation. For my own sanity, I finally had to release the need to know why. While it feels like a massive betrayal of loyalty, I will likely never know what happened.

You don't always get closure and your willingness to accept that begins the healing process. You may never get an apology or a chance to say that brilliant response you've been rehearsing. Don Henley is one of my all-time favorite lyricists. He has a great song entitled *My Thanksgiving* (*YouTube* it!) and I quote: "Have you ever noticed that an angry man can only get so far - until he reconciles the way he thinks things ought to be with the way things are." Forgiveness doesn't diminish the violation; it just frees you up to live your life unencumbered. I can assure you they're not thinking about YOU! No longer do you have to give your personal power away to someone else.

Bringing It Home

Perhaps hardest of all, contentment comes on a grander scale from forgiving *ourselves*. Ponder where you might be holding your own atonement for ransom. It's time to forgive yourself for not finishing your degree or for burning the Thanksgiving turkey. Forgive yourself for marrying the wrong person or forgetting your sister's birthday. Forgive yourself for not being a perfect housekeeper or not recognizing a loved one's illness before it was too late. Forgive yourself for abusing your body and mismanaging your finances. Life is a constant evolution of screwing up and learning and getting smarter. Every day is a new opportunity for us to cut ourselves some much deserved slack!

As we learn to think of our imperfections as mirrors into our beliefs, we can use them, one at a time, to create a better experience and give ourselves reasons to be proud. As I mentioned before, in my coaching practice, there's a common thread of belief pervasive in almost every woman I've ever worked with. It's the subconscious misnomer that we are inherently broken in some way and we'll be okay as soon as we fix that "thing" that keeps us from being whole and lovable. Each of us has our own "thing" based on our history. Here are a few samples of the stories I've heard:

I'll be okay when I…

- Finish my degree
- Lose fifty pounds
- Find my life partner
- Get out of this job
- Make peace with my mom
  (or fill in the blank)
- Save enough money
- Discover my life purpose
- Etc. Etc. Etc.

The myth of the superwoman is really the belief that we have to be skilled at everything, that we must exhibit consistent work/life balance, nurture our relationships, grow organic vegetables for our breakfast smoothies, clock 30 miles a day on the Peloton and look damn good doing it! While we instinctively know how ludicrous that perception is, we still spend countless time, energy, and money trying to live up to that ideal, don't we?

The nature of being human is expansion. You will always want to be more than you *are* because growing is why you're here. By accepting yourself exactly as you are right now, you will come to merely *observe* your mistakes rather than *be defined by* them, you can then draw on them for personal growth. Remember that we're all doing the best we can with the information we have. Hindsight allows us to make better decisions for the next chance we get.

BLISS BREAK:
When you're ready to create more peace in your life, take a deep breath, grab a pen and your journal. Give yourself a big giant bear hug and tackle these questions I've leveraged from Katherine Woodward Thomas' incredible book, *Calling in the One*.

Repeat this exercise with everyone you feel you need to forgive (or at least quit thinking about).

Releasing Resentment

Who am I carrying resentment toward?

What do I resent this person for?

What can I be responsible for in this situation?

In what ways can this experience help me to become a more mature person?

What lessons did I learn?

What good can come of this situation?

What have I been unwilling to accept about this situation?

What can I now let go of, so the situation is complete?

The point here is not to try and make sense of your past or even get others to give you the closure you so desperately crave. If you want, it can be very cathartic to write a letter to the person(s) you believed have wronged you. You don't even need to send the letter. Write it and release it. I enjoy a good ceremonial burning bowl or swirly "burial at sea" to get my own closure. (Prosecco or cookie dough ice cream accompaniment are completely optional, but highly recommended.)

"Free at last! Free at last! Thank God Almighty, you're free at last!"

Chapter 7
Synchronicity

I do believe in an everyday sort of magic -- the inexplicable connectedness we sometimes experience with places, people, works of art and the like; the eerie appropriateness of moments of **synchronicity**; *the whispered voice, the hidden presence, when we think we're alone.*
- Carl Jung, Founder of Analytical Psychology

Have you noticed when you're actively in the flow of joy, your life seems to be a series of fun coincidences and little surprises? Bliss isn't something you achieve. It's something you *allow*. You can't set a goal of happiness because it's not a task. It isn't about making your Instagram look like a Hallmark commercial. It's about finding those little nuggets of joy living stealthily in the everyday. Giving your conscious attention to those simple moments creates a proclivity to happiness. This isn't just positive thinking. It's more like positive *observation*, combined with taking an active role in creating an environment more pleasing to you in every way.

Synchronicity can show up in the smallest of ways. In fact, if you're not paying attention, you may miss these tiny delights. It can feel like you're just in the right place at the right time. You may find a five-dollar bill blowing through the parking lot just when you've realized you forgot to get cash to pay the meter or you stop by a church rummage sale where you find the exact same wine stem you broke last week. When we pay attention, we realize what may feel like random coincidences are really the Universe reacting to our thoughts, circumstances, and beliefs.

You Must Be Present to Win

I had the great pleasure a while back to dine at the home of the brilliant and hospitable Ken Blanchard, leadership guru and super nice guy. After a glorious meal, we retired to the family room where he and his wife gifted us with the opportunity to ask them questions. Most memorably, someone asked him how he became so wildly successful in a time when everyone had similar offerings. Without hesitation, he responded, "I simply kept my head up, so I could see. While everyone was heads down doing the work, I was watching people's reactions and what was going on around me." These enjoyable non-events happen to you all the time, but you need to have your head up in order to notice them. The average person has about sixty to seventy thousand thoughts a day and the technology we invented to simplify our lives basically owns us now. So, between our own monkey chatter and external stimuli, it's no surprise we struggle to be present with the awesomeness going on around us.

I saw the most enlightening TEDx Talk a while back by Matthew Killingsworth, a clinical psychologist who studies the nature and causes of human happiness. In his research around "Cognitive Mind Wandering" with over 650,000 data points, he showed us some interesting facts. For example, 55% of the time, you're thinking about something *other* than what you're doing! While it's possible for mind wandering to occasionally result in creativity and innovation, here's the truth: within 1-3 mins after mind wandering, people were infinitely *less* happy than they were before they mentally ventured from the task at hand, no matter what they were doing. So, what's that about? When your mind is wandering, are you thinking about unicorns and butterflies and rainbows? Yeah…no. Most of the time, our musings are filled with anxiety, fear, regret, and frustration.

The majority of the time, we are thinking about what we *don't* want and can't figure out why we keep getting it. In fact, Brene Brown goes so far as to say we "dress rehearse tragedy" so we're not disappointed when it happens. That's so twisted, yet we do it. As Dr. Phil would say, "How's that workin' for you?"

Law of Attraction 101

This is basic Law of Attraction stuff. I don't have to go into the research supporting this concept. There are plenty of people writing about this. What you think about always expands and it's been scientifically proven over and over since before we began capturing words on paper. I'm not a biblical scholar, but this is not a new realization. "For as a man thinketh in his heart, so is he…" (Proverbs 23:7). Some other historical text may have started this revelation thousands of years ago and it has been reinforced by countless studies since then. The medical industry recognizes the absolute importance of one's thinking in the healing process. Professional athletes have been leveraging the power of conscious and subconscious thought for centuries. I've had enough experience in my own life and that of my clients to know these small and large miracles are no coincidence.

This is Supposed to be FUN!

I encourage you not to take this practice too seriously. The creative process is the best game ever! Try not to make it arduous. It's not your job to *make* things happen. Just set the intention to be open and receptive. The first few times you notice it, you'll be amazed and mildly suspicious. But once you get in the practice (and it does take practice) of positive expectation, these events will be your norm.

Positive expectation simply means you go through your day expecting good things to happen versus worrying or waiting for the other shoe to fall. It's about visioning what your life will look like when you have what you want. The more specific you can get with your vision, the more likely you are to recognize it when it shows up in your life. I still get tickled when synchronicities occur, I'm just not surprised anymore.

I can cite so many personal instances, yet there are a few of my favorites I'd love to share because they were too specific to be random.

<u>The Sewage Cap Story</u>

I'm fairly certain there has never been a story published with this title, which is why the experience was so significant. Before my daughter began driving, her Dad and I lived at opposite ends of the city, so we split the drive during her visitations. Halfway for us was a mostly unused exit off a low traffic highway. There were no buildings there. It was wooded and quiet. The only reason there was an exit was to have access to a lake several miles down the road. We would just pull under the overpass and make the kid swap.

One Sunday morning, I decided I need to try and get my yard mowed before I left to pick her up. It was going to be tight, but I was on a mission. In my frenzy to get done, I accidentally mowed over the outdoor sewage cap and sheared the whole top off. (It was one of those white round PVC caps with the little square on top.) I was irritated with myself for rushing. Worried rodents would get inside, I stuck a coffee can over it and jumped in the car to get my daughter.

I was thinking about that stupid cap all the way there and how I didn't have time for this. As I exited, I was distracted looking for her dad's car and almost ran over an obstacle in the road that would have done significant tire damage. I swerved to miss it. Glancing out the window, I was stunned to see (you guessed it) a brand new, with the sticker still on it, gleaming white sewage cap exactly the size I needed. There was seriously no reason for it to be out there in the middle of nowhere. No construction anywhere nearby. In fact, no people for miles. I probably should have made it into a shadow box. But it lives in my yard as a reminder that "thoughts are things."

The Silver Lining

One more for posterity...
I wholeheartedly admit I have a jewelry problem. I just love it, especially sterling silver. Perhaps it's only a trend, but I would kill now to have all the turquoise and silver jewelry I sold at a garage sale back in the late 70s. I've been particularly partial to a brand called Silpada because they were our local girls gone international. I loved their story and I love their jewelry. One of my first purchases was a pair of pounded silver hoops I wore pretty much every day, with everything. On a brief business trip, I proceeded to leave them in my hotel, never to be located again. I was super bummed because they weren't cheap and more pressing things were vying for my income at the time. I lamented them daily during my morning routine.

Meanwhile, I walked my daughter to school every day (until she forbade me in sixth grade). The long, curved driveway was always an endless line of cars dropping their kids off. It was an interesting challenge for pedestrians to navigate through. One morning, it had been raining and we were both excited to premiere our matching butterfly galoshes. Not missing a puddle, we made our way up the hill and through the parking lot. Assured the blue Honda had waved us through, we trotted in front of it. Almost to the other side, my daughter noticed a puddle she had somehow missed and took two steps back to hit it square. When she did, something splashed out of the puddle and onto my boot. It was a tiny plastic Ziploc bag containing (how are you still surprised?) a brand-new version of the same hammered earrings that I had lost! The bag contained an invoice with what turned out to have a bogus name and phone number. With all the integrity I could muster, I left them at the front desk to be claimed. After two weeks, the office called me and told me to pick them up.

I don't question it anymore. I just say, "thank you." How fun it is when you find a nugget of fabulosity in the middle of your routine daily tasks! But you have to be open to veering off course a bit in order to experience the wonderment. Albert Einstein said it best,

If we decide that the Universe is neither friendly nor unfriendly and that God is essentially 'playing dice with the Universe, then we are simply victims to the random toss of the dice and our lives have no real purpose or meaning.

He was alluding to his belief that you can predict the overall happiness of your life by how you answer one question: Is this a friendly Universe? If you get up every day thinking it's you against the world, you're going to spend your day pushing a chain uphill and miss your magic moments. But if you believe you came here with the resources and love you need to be successful the stars will align. The right people will show up. Opportunities arise and you have a choice as to whether or not you're going to play.

BLISS BREAK:
If you've been out of practice for a while, here are some suggestions for being more present and awake to the synchronicities in your life. Check them off as you give each a try.

Making Magic

o Set an intention to manifest something really small like a free cup of coffee or a rock star parking spot. Then visualize it several times a day and just expect it to be there.

o Set the timer on your phone to go off every hour or two. Take 60 seconds each time to be completely present. Notice everything around you. What's on your desk? Who's in your space? How are you feeling? What does your body want?

o Practice the activity above using all of your senses without judgment. What do you smell right now? What do you hear? What do you see? Notice the texture of whatever's in your hands.

o Make mindfulness a habit. This may come in the form of meditation. If you aren't great at sitting still, take a walk and be cognizant of what's around you. If you can't quiet your thinking, use a mindfulness app on your phone or listen to a guided meditation that directs you.

Making Magic cont.

- Reduce distractions. Eliminate background noise like TV while you're working. Create a designated space and time for quiet.

- Journal. To chronicle your day, you have to recall it. You'll be amazed when things happen down the road you attribute to coincidence or luck, but when you look back at your own writing, you realize you created it first in your thoughts and forgot about it.

- Celebrate the tiny joys, everything from bumping into a friend to finding a killer recipe on Pinterest. Acknowledging the small goodness attracts more of it to you.

- Recognize a trigger and change that habit. If you feel stressed and over-caffeinated, trade one cup each day for an herbal tea or try half decaf. If as soon as you get to work, all your plans are scrapped by other people's requests, establish what your top three goals are for the day and be willing to work the needs of others around those top three.

Most of us are sleepwalking through life and we're completely missing the things that make life worth getting out of bed for. A conscious shift in awareness, if even for a few moments a day, will be life changing. Bottom line: Wake up and smell the magic!

Chapter 8
Expectancy

The world will meet us at our level of expectancy.
– Tony Robbins, Self-help Guru and Author

People don't always do what we want them to do, but they almost always show up the way we *expect* them to. There is a ton of research that indicates how unconscious bias impacts not only our performance and relationships, but overall happiness. It's all tied directly to our core underlying beliefs about the world and the people we encounter.

Remember the Confirmation Bias

The concept of confirmation bias is the well-proven theory that we seek out evidence to support what we already believe to be true. The first psychologist to systematically study this was a Harvard professor named Robert Rosenthal, who in 1964 did an experiment at an elementary school in San Francisco. The idea was to figure out what would happen if teachers were told that certain kids in their class were destined to succeed, so Rosenthal took a standardized IQ test and dressed it up with a different cover. He told the teachers that this very special test from Harvard had the ability to predict which kids were gifted—that is, which kids were about to experience a dramatic growth in their IQ. After they took the assessment, he then chose from every class several children totally at random. There was nothing at all to distinguish these kids from the other kids, but he told their teachers that the test predicted these kids were on the verge of an intense intellectual bloom.

As he followed the children over the next two years, Rosenthal discovered that the teachers' expectations of the chosen kids very much affected the outcome. How? The research found that expectations affect teachers' moment-to-moment interactions with the children in multiple subtle ways. Teachers give the students they expected to succeed more time to answer questions, more specific feedback, and more approval. They consistently touch, nod, and smile at those kids more. As a result, they naturally showed greater growth. Obviously, this sort of study is pretty messed up and would never be done today, but let's get the lesson here.

If you're wondering how this is relevant to you, I want you to consider the story you are telling about who you are and what's possible for you and others. What are the things you most commonly say about those closest to you? Are you expecting people to disappoint you? Are you always waiting for the other shoe to fall? Whether you call it confirmation bias or self-fulfilling prophecy, our expectations serve as the container for our life experiences. It's also how we train others to treat us.

It's been proven over and over how critical our beliefs are in shaping the world around us. Think of it like pouring concrete. Your manifestations will always take the shape of the mold that's created. And if you leave your beliefs there long enough, they'll harden and create a right sturdy foundation for how you operate in the world.

Bliss Tip: *The best way to battle confirmation bias is to challenge your thought as it starts to upset you. You do this by searching for evidence that's counter to what you're believing in the moment.*

Example about YOU:
You have to take a business trip the week of your daughter's dance recital. You're thinking, "I'm a terrible mom. I should always be there for my kids."

Your challenge now is to recount all the times that you chauffeured the Girl Scouts and kissed boo-boos and read your kids to sleep as evidence that you are not really a terrible parent.

Example about ANOTHER:
Your husband comes home tired from work, grabs a beer out of the fridge, and retires to the tv without really acknowledging you. You're thinking, "He doesn't care about me. The romance is gone."

Your challenge now is to recount the small, unsung things he does all the time to show he cares, like starting the coffee in the morning for you, washing your car, little forehead kisses before you fall asleep, or bragging about you to his friends.

City of Cowards

I live in the Greater Kansas City area. I ran into someone recently who is an avid historian and was relaying to me an interesting story about my hometown. During the Gold Rush days, KC was commonly known as the "City of Cowards." Needless to say, that's not been my experience, so I was intrigued by the history. Apparently, news spread quickly of the gold in the hills of California. Turns out, at the time, Kansas City was the last stop on the Santa Fe-California-Oregon Trail before you began the arduous and dangerous trek across the badlands, through the Rocky Mountains and barren desert. Many didn't survive. The trip was treacherous and a lot of people either starved to death or fell ill on the journey. So, it wasn't uncommon for folks to get as far as KC, look at the risk ahead and think, "You know, this is a nice town. I think I'm good." And many just stayed and homesteaded here.

As I listened to him tell this story, I couldn't help but wonder how people's beliefs about the risk influenced whether they chose to go on and if the new wealthy just *expected* to make it safely to the promised land filled with gold.

Chapter 9
Connection

Each person we meet represents a world in us, a world possibly not born until they arrive, and it is only by this meeting that a new world is born.
  – Anais Nin, French-Cuban Erotica Novelist

I don't want to bum you out, but the global reality is depression has increased ten-fold since 1989. While there are myriad contributors playing into this statistic—not the least of which are screen sucking, poor diet, and swipe dating—but the number one reason cited by a positive psychology study at the University of Pennsylvania is unanimously "lack of connectedness to something bigger than ourselves". Happiness is directly linked to relationships, both interpersonal planetary relationships and with your non-physical support system—whatever beliefs float your spiritual boat. I'm a God girl, but you don't need to be to feel the loneliness of universal misalignment. The area of connection is where I see the most obvious barrier to bliss.

The Happiness Index

Recently, I found myself locked onto a Marie Forleo interview with Dan Buettner, a National Geographic Fellow who has traveled the world studying human happiness. His mission is capturing the factors that predict joy and he's created an index to measure it. The pinnacle of his findings can be summed up in his one statement:

One of the biggest predictors of whether you'll be happy on a day-to-day basis is how many hours of face time you have with people you like.

Notice he specifies it should be people you truly enjoy being around. Connection doesn't happen just because there are people around you. We've all had the experience of being lonely in a crowd. Bliss happens when you are having what Dr. Edward Hallowell calls "a human moment." The human moment has two prerequisites—your physical presence and your emotional and intellectual attention. That's it. Physical presence alone isn't enough; you can ride shoulder-to-shoulder with someone for six hours in an airplane and not have a human moment. Connection requires you be totally present with the other person(s). You're not looking at your phone or judging each other's motives. You're just listening with genuine interest and enjoying the moment with all your senses.

Coming Home

I'm reminded of the story of a married middle-aged couple driving to dinner in their old bench-seat pickup truck. The wife looks longingly across the truck at her husband and says, "Honey, remember when we used to sit right next to each other and cuddle whenever we drove to dinner? What has happened to us?" The husband just glanced over at his frustrated wife and smiled. Then he sarcastically replies, "I haven't moved."
I love this story so much because it reflects where we create our own disconnects. We do it with those closest to us by being self-involved and "busy." We become more focused on the tasks than who we are doing them for in the first place.

Healing at the Red Racks

Bliss can be found when our interpersonal sensitivity is on hyper-alert. It's super simple. It just means you notice the people around you and genuinely respond to them. If someone smiles at you, you smile back. If someone looks sad or mad, you smile first. If you admire someone's outfit or they have beautiful eyes, you tell them (not in a creepy way).

I was looking for a piece of furniture to refinish, so I stopped at a local Red Racks Thrift Store. There was a young twenty-something guy working the counter. He was tall and very slender with John Lennon glasses and a tiny blond man-bun atop his head. I watched the care he took with the two elderly people in line in front of me, his patience as he helped a man count money, how he complimented a woman's hair, and offered a big smile and a wave as people filtered in.

I acknowledged his kindness when I got up to the register and he just said, "That last woman's husband just had a stroke and she gets frustrated. And the man over there is 92 and he's raising three of his great grandkids. Sometimes folks just come in to have somebody to talk to." I paid for my stuff. As I walked away, I said, "I hope you know how important the work is you're doing." He just smiled at me and nodded.

So much healing happening in the world if you're paying attention. So much need for connection and nothing is more fulfilling than initiating that touch point.

Bliss Tip: *Quality time with another doesn't mean you spend hours gazing into each other's eyes or sacrificing your needs for another. Just find something to do together that you both enjoy – and leave your phone in the other room. It doesn't matter what the activity is. What happens on the emotional level is what matters. People are starved for that human moment. Give yourself the gift of connection at some point every day.*

<u>*Pay It Forward*</u>

I stopped at the Hen House grocery store recently to grab some last-minute stuff for dinner. I just had a handful of items, so I wandered over to the express lane. There was just one woman in line in front of me. From all appearances, she was homeless. She was maybe my age, but her face showed decades of stress. Her hair was tangled and tied loosely with a dirty bandana. Her clothes were mismatched and layered heavily for a July day, like she was wearing everything she owned at once. She had three things in her basket: a loaf of white bread, a bar of Dial soap, and a 20 oz. Diet Coke.

For context, I have to back up about twenty minutes in my story to the drive-thru at Starbucks in the same parking lot. I had ordered a tall Mocha Lite Frappuccino. I pulled up to the window to pay for my drink, only to find that the car in front of me had already paid for mine. Oh, happy day! I felt like I'd won the coffee lottery. Smiling and sipping my winnings, I drove to the aforementioned grocery store…

As I waited in the express lane, the homeless woman pulled out two one-dollar bills and some change from her pocket and told the clerk, "Hold off on the Diet Coke to see if I have enough money." With my free coffee still in my hand, I told her that someone had just gifted me a beverage and I'd love to pay it forward and buy her Diet Coke for her. She was stunned and gratefully accepted my offer. Then she said, "One day I hope to be able to pay it forward."

Still checking out, I watched the woman head toward the door, but she stopped suddenly beside a small boy who was sitting on the stationary dinosaur ride. He was sad because he wanted to ride, but his mom didn't have any change. The homeless woman reached in her pocket, pulled out a quarter, and put it in the slot to start the ride. The little guy's face lit up and he thanked her. She turned and looked at me and winked. She had already paid it forward.

It's a Girl Thang

I love men. I do. I was raised the only girl with three brothers, whom I deeply adore. Growing up in a house full of boys taught me three things:

1. I am always looked out for.
2. It is possible to laugh so hard Dr. Pepper comes out your nose.
3. NEVER "smell this."

All very important life lessons I learned from the men in my life.

But what I underestimated for most of my life is the value of a solid tribe of women friends who supported and believed in me. When I moved into the workforce a bazillion years ago, there were not the same opportunities available to women that we have now. It was a very competitive market and I learned early, the hard way, that women were not to be trusted. We were taught to fight for the better jobs, the good men, and any sort of credibility.

Fortunately, great strides have been made to lessen the discrepancy in the workplace. And I'm beyond thrilled to have lived to see the day where women hold each other up and value the bond we share as a gender. I tell my daughter frequently that intimate relationships will come and go. Jobs will make promises that get broken. But your girls-they're forever. Build a strong network of loving, authentic, and confident women and you will never again be alone.

The Myth of the Superwoman

I spent my entire adult life convincing myself that I didn't need to rely on anyone but myself—to raise my kid, for financial support, or to make me happy. So, I proved I could do it. Big damn deal. There was no fanfare, no one cheering me from the sidelines. All I had proven is that I could survive being alone.
I had plenty of friends and respected colleagues, yet none of them were with me in the middle of the night when my daughter was throwing up or sharing the burden of worry that I carried as a single mom. How nice it would have been to reach out to a willing support system. It's not that my friends wouldn't have helped. They totally would have. But I sent out the clear message that I was just fine, thank you very much. I am woman. Hear me roar. What I wouldn't give to have a do-over on that period of my life–to have the joy of sisterhood and a little more sanity. No woman is an island. Who knew?

Bliss Tip: *There's a payoff for every distorted belief we harbor and story of woe we tell. Being a single mom was a great excuse to relieve me from a lot of stuff I didn't want to own. I used it to get out of social events. And it's a fairly legitimate alibi for why my hair was in a ponytail or my house wasn't clean, or I didn't have the money. Take a look at your wonky beliefs—the ones that no longer serve you—and get honest with yourself about what your payoff has been. Until you're ready to release the need for the excuses, you'll struggle to let go of your old story.*

Through whatever trauma or drama you may live through, you can call on your tribe and they will be right there. We all need a variety of chicas in our life for our various circumstances. You know which friend will commiserate with you and tell you you're absolutely justified in hanging up on their sorry ass and polishing off a full tube of snickerdoodle cookie dough. Then you have the friend who'll tell you to put on your big girl panties and get over it. If you're lucky, you'll also have the friend who'll just hold you while you cry and not say a word. There's the gal who inspires you to work harder and the one who forces you to slow down and relax. They're all equally fabulous and irreplaceable. Build your tribe (and I don't just mean on-line), I mean real people you can touch and feel their energy. You won't regret it.

Go Outside!

Finally, I can't *not* mention the inherent connection we all share with the Earth. The average lifestyle has shifted to a more sedentary, indoor existence. It's been said that sitting is the new smoking. The invention of the personal computer keeps people in unnatural, debilitating positions for hours under artificial lighting. As a result, by the end of the day, we feel like someone has pulled the plug and drained the entire life force out of our bodies.

Perhaps the idea of camping in the wilderness makes your skin crawl. You don't have to be a survivalist to leverage the benefits of a little fresh air and greenscape. I was watching Nickelodeon with my daughter years back and a young guy came on to do a public service announcement. He was talking about the growing popularity of video games and virtual reality. Then he said, "I know they're fun, but I have a new idea, kids: how about ACTUAL reality? Go outside!" It cracked us both up. We immediately turned off the TV and went out to dust the cobwebs off our bikes.

There are sounds and smells and colors and textures you can only find outdoors, things that soothe your soul and remind you that you are connected with this planet and everything on it. You're never alone… and nature proves that to you.

BLISS BREAK: The 30-Day Connection Challenge

For 30 days in a row, set yourself the goal to connect with at least one person in a meaningful way. It doesn't have to cost money or take much time or even be philanthropic. It just has to be genuine. Consider the list below and hold yourself accountable to actually making the contact. This is your commitment to more human moments. It feels <u>SO GOOD</u>! And while you will be doing this from a place of pure giving, it's impossible not to reap the natural benefits of making deposits into people.

On the next page I've provided you with a list of possible ways to reach out. But get creative. Do whatever inspires you.
At the end of it all, the people in your life are the only thing that ever really mattered. Another fav Don Henley quote,

> "You don't see no hearses with luggage racks."

1. Invite someone to lunch today.
2. Pay for someone's coffee/beverage.
3. Call someone you haven't talked to in 6 months.
4. Make eye contact and smile at a stranger.
5. Take cookies to a neighbor.
6. Thank a co-worker.
7. Send someone a card in the mail.
8. Buy a dozen flowers and give one to random people who look like they could use one.
9. Cook with someone (or for someone).
10. Take leftovers to someone single or homebound.
11. Take a walk with somebody.
12. Share an article or podcast that would be of interest to someone.
13. Loan a favorite book.
14. Mentor someone.
15. Send a random funny selfie (or a Bitmoji).
16. If someone looks like they need help, offer (reach high on a shelf or open a door).
17. Be the first to apologize.
18. Do something romantic.
19. Be generous with hugs.
20. Seek first to understand before you try to prove yourself right.
21. Bring donuts for no reason.
22. Offer a genuine compliment.
23. Sit on the porch with a glass of iced tea and wave at passersby.
24. Volunteer.
25. Organize a block party or movie night on your garage door.
26. Dust the cobwebs off your bike.
27. Start a book club (knitting club, walking group, business pow-wow).
28. Put doggie snacks and water on the sidewalk for walking pups.
29. Put together hygiene/snack packs from hotel soaps to keep in your car for the homeless you see. Quart size Ziplocs work well.
30. Have a picnic in the park.

Chapter 10
Play

We don't stop playing because we get old; we get old because we stop playing.
- George Bernard Shaw, Winner of the Nobel Prize for Literature

It's time to let go of exhaustion as a status symbol and productivity as a trophy for self-worth. I know it's so much easier to say than it is to live. I was raised in a big Irish family. We were always playing pranks on each other. My Mom had all four of her kids by the time she was 22, so we pretty much grew up together with our parents. As a result, play was our norm. Our home décor was blacklight posters and fishnet on the ceiling. (It was the 60s, okay?)

I remember one Thanksgiving, we didn't have the money for a turkey, but hamburger was nineteen cents a pound. My Mom bought three pounds of burger, made a meatloaf and shaped it like a turkey. My dad sliced it sideways. Often my parents couldn't pay the utilities and the lights were shut off. My Dad created a murder mystery game that we played throughout the house with flashlights. We thought it was hilarious. I didn't know we were poor until I got into high school and realized not everyone looked under the sofa cushions for change so they could buy bread for sandwiches. Play was born of necessity for us, but it not only showed me how to do a great deal with nothing, it also taught me not to take things so seriously.

Act as If

There's a prestigious neighborhood in greater Kansas City known as Mission Hills. It boasts gorgeous meandering homes and is said to be one of the wealthiest areas in the country, most famous for housing Ernest Hemingway in 1928 when he wrote *A Farewell to Arms*. My dad was a dreamer. Every Sunday, he would pile his herd into our old rusty Rambler Station Wagon with no exhaust pipe. Our favorite game was cruising Mission Hills, pretending to pick our future houses. I'm certain people would lock their doors when we drove by. My pick was a Spanish Tudor high on a hill, with a waterfall cascading through the side yard. But it had navy blue awnings. I thought they were tacky, so I decided when I took ownership, those awnings had to go! It was a joyous game that entertained us for hours. The cherry on top was a trip afterward to the tamale truck in front of the Sears Outlet. Besides being mega-fun, these outings taught us that life has no limitations and that where you come from doesn't have to have any bearing on where you're going.

Ironic addendum to this story: About a year ago, I moved into what would best be described as a carriage house in a nearby neighborhood. Yet, when I pull up Google Weather, it shows my location as Mission Hills. Guess I finally made it, Daddy. Cheers!

Do You Remember How to Play?

Adulting can sometimes wean the playful right out of us, so you may need a nudge for how to spontaneously and joyfully play. I'm happy to share some of my favs with you during this next Bliss Break.

BLISS BREAK: Everyday ways to play with your kids –

- Cook with them. Google is full of recipes on how to make a hot dog octopus or Rice Crispie eyeballs.
- Put water in anything and let them play in it. As long as they're wet, they're happy.
- Make collages. Grab a bunch of magazines, scrapbooking paper, stickers, scissors, and glue sticks. You're never too old to cut and paste.
- Sing and dance. Crank the tunes when it's time to clean house. Sock puppets make great dusters and picking up toys happens much faster when it's a race.
- Get physical. Nothing more fun than the tickle monster, a pillow fight, or a reckless ride down the hall in a laundry basket.
- Let them read to you. At age 16, my daughter read me the entire Hunger Games series one chapter every night before bed (okay, sometimes two chapters if I couldn't stand the suspense).

The Love Troll

I used to date a guy who lived in St. Louis, which was a four-hour drive from me. Twice a month we'd take turns making the cross-state trek. One year we went to the Soulard Mardi Gras where we won a tiny troll doll, you know, the kind with all the hair and big belly that are so ugly, they're cute? I wrote *"ILY"* on his little belly and we called him the *"Love Troll"*. When I left to go home that weekend, he handed the troll to me to take home.

I said, "No, I think he wants to live here with you."

To which he responded, "No…I'm pretty sure he'd be happier at your house."

I set him back on his dining table, but when I got home, the love troll had found its way mysteriously into my suitcase. My next trip back, I put the doll inside his toilet paper roll. So, the next year and a half became a full-on stealth challenge to find creative ways to make sure the other person ended up with the love troll. He was frozen in an ice cube tray, folded into an umbrella, shipped to a NY hotel during a business trip. It became a hilarious and wildly competitive game for us and still one of my fondest memories.

BLISS BREAK: Everyday ways to play with your Honey –

- Leave a loaded Nerf gun on the dining room table with a note that reads, "Hi Babe. Welcome home. Two Things: 1) This gun with ammo is yours. 2) I'm hiding in the house. I have one, too. You are under attack as of right now." When you see him pull up, go hide. Game on!
- Pet names are always a favorite. Just make sure you don't use it for anyone else. If you're one of those people who calls everyone "honey" or "babe," find something more specific and personal for your *lovah*.
- Play hooky from work and meet in the middle of a weekday for a movie or a winery or *whatever*.
- Do a Cosmo quiz together.
- Arrange a surprise overnight with a theme just slightly out of town. Pack for them and tell them you're going someplace boring, like a business dinner and then just drive until they get suspicious.
- Make a sizzling sex video. Actually, reconsider that – It may show up on *60 Minutes* when you're famous.

FYWN

A lifetime ago, the weekend my daughter's dad re-married was going to be a tough one for me. Mariah was a four-year-old flower girl and excited about the dress and the job. I didn't want to squelch her enthusiasm, but it was honestly the last thing I wanted to be continuously talking about for the two weeks prior. I was going to be alone in my house without her, trying desperately not to think about what was happening across town. But only moments after he picked her up, there was another knock on my door. I opened it to the sight of five of my best girlfriends in matching pink cowgirl hats and lime green t-shirts with the letters painted: "*FYWN.*" What the...?

They told me to pack an overnight bag and tossed me my own green shirt to put on. I asked what was up, but couldn't get a straight answer, so I just got in the car. They drove me to a buffalo ranch and resort about a half hour out of town where we stayed at a gorgeous bed and breakfast. The staff greeted us with frozen margaritas and fresh baked chips. Turns out, the FYWN stands for "F**k You, Who's Next?" This was an intervention to keep me from being sad and alone during a really difficult time. They had prepared skits and gag gifts. I laughed 'til I cried for two days. It was the best.

Beyond the Happy Hour

For most of us, even the smallest amount of time with good friends is the prescription for most anything that ails you. I did however notice that I had gotten into a pattern somehow of all of my get-togethers revolving around food and/or liquor in a public venue. Maybe that's the easiest to schedule, but I was finding it kind of boring to do all the time - not to mention expensive. I ask myself what happened to the days when friends just dropped in for an iced tea on the deck or a game of Yahtzee. I longed for the evenings spent with friends that didn't involve putting on makeup or whipping out the American Express. So, I suggested to my closest friends that we get creative and think of other things to do besides happy hour. I was amazed at the thought people put into it and relieved at the relaxed nature of our connects. One friend invited me over mid-week to paint river rocks on her back porch. I threw on some sweats, brought a bottle of vino and she had easy snacks. It was great to catch up and the painting was very therapeutic. Another friend encouraged me to join her Jazzercise class, so we get to chat and get a workout in together twice a week.

BLISS BREAK: Everyday ways to play with your Friends –

- Think of creative ways to hang out together that don't involve liquor or food. Go paddle-boarding. Paint a mug at a ceramic shop. Hike. Take a cooking class. Hit the park swings and just catch up.
- Have private jokes. Savor those moments when you both start giggling and no one knows why, and they think you've lost your mind.
- Play Cards Against Humanity or Vertellis
- Play a Team Sport. Recreational volleyball or softball or Frisbee golf create camaraderie, so long as you can keep the competitiveness on the down low.
- Host a Murder Mystery party.
- Buy matching duckie jammies and wear them to the drive-in.

Time Off from Adulting

I was mega-inspired by Joan Anderson's book, *A Weekend to Change Your Life*. I read it during a period of extreme chaos in my life. It was actually a very timely read. She tells the story of how she basically went on strike. She left her family for a solid year to retreat on Cape Cod to get to know herself again. Being my only source of income, checking out for a year wasn't an option for me (or most anyone), but I decided I could swing a week. I have several clients in Massachusetts. I'm familiar with the area and I thought it would be fun to socialize and network while I was there. I bought a non-refundable ticket and rented an Airbnb in Chatham, so I couldn't back out. This turned out to be the most irrational and wonderful thing I've ever done for myself.

Best laid plans aside, something about the salt air and the cozy cabin seduced me into doing absolutely nothing productive all week long. I never put on make-up (I *did* shower), but I didn't see another soul I knew all week. I cooked breakfast and lunch at the cabin and ate every dinner at a different restaurant on the water. Then I strolled, hypnotized by the waves until it got too dark. I slept in and turned off my social media. One night, I ate a whole bag of coconut jelly beans while I watched shark week until midnight. Every once in a blue moon, you have to quit adulting and just *be*.

BLISS BREAK: Everyday ways to play with Yourself - that won't make you blind (*while I have no argument against that either*) –

- Skip rocks.
- Dance around your house in your underwear to Grace & the Nocturnals' *Hot Summer Nights.*
- Paint your toenails all in a different color.
- Make yourself chocolate chip pancakes. (Bonus points if you shape them like a Disney character)
- Watch *P.S. I Love You* with a large box of tissues. (Bonus points if you do a shot every time you see Gerard Butler's abs)
- Collect something.
- Learn a good magic trick that you can show off.
- Make a Donny Osmond playlist.
- Put a temporary pink (or blue or purple) streak in your hair.
- Walk downtown and do an urban photo shoot of unexpected things.
- The possibilities are endless...

It's All Life

Even as an adult, when interviewing for a job, I'd always ask, "What do you guys do for fun around here?" If they look at me like I have a horn growing out of my forehead, then I already know it's not a good match. Companies who value play have a higher retention rate and better productivity than those who are nose to the grind-stone. Opt for the businesses who have *Bring your dog to work Friday* or reward innovation over compliance. In fact, I would argue that the opposite of play isn't work—it's despair. When we no longer play, we've given up on the belief that life wasn't meant to be a struggle.

I saw an interview with Sir Richard Branson. You know the guy - all things Virgin (Virgin Airlines, Virgin Mobile, Virgin Music…). He kind of has a reputation for being a playful sort. Someone asked him what percentage of time he spent playing versus working. He looked a little perplexed and responded, "I don't think of it as work or play. To me, it's all life." I think that's brilliant advice. You see, when you do anything you love with people you enjoy, the line is blurred.

Chapter 11
Ritual

Ritual reminds us that ordinary life is sacred.
- Jane Austin, English Novelist

Family and social rituals usually start early in life, which is important because these rituals shape our view of how the world should operate—everything from rights-of-passage to holiday meals and just general family dynamics. But as we outgrow our childhood rituals, there's still an inherent need to maintain that connection to the magic and safety that comes with familiarity.

Webster's defines RITUAL AS "a sequence of activities involving gestures, words, and objects, often performed according to set sequence." Over time, we've come to associate it with religious traditions, but ceremony is actually crucial to the whole human experience when it comes to building relationships and just maintaining our sanity!

Ceremony with a Purpose

People engage in rituals with the intention of achieving a wide array of desired outcomes—reducing anxiety, boosting confidence, alleviating grief, or performing well in a competition... or even making it rain. You hear stories all the time about athletes who have little habits they've adopted that they believe play into their success. Michael Jordan used to always wear his NC shorts under his Chicago Bulls uniform for good luck. If you've seen the movie *Bull Durham*, you'll recall Tim Robbins wears his girlfriend's underwear every game because he thinks that's what's responsible for his pitching streak! So, Kevin Costner (who plays his coach) just rolls with it... "Rosette goes in the front, big guy!" Our beliefs play a massive role in our success, so creating positive rituals will always foster feelings of optimism and comfort. That's why we do it.

In fact, recent studies suggest that rituals may be more rational than they appear. Even simple routines can be extremely effective. Rituals performed after experiencing significant loss really does alleviate grief. You'll see people get commemorative tattoos or run yearly marathons to honor a loved one. And rituals performed before high-pressure tasks – like singing in public or taking a test– do in fact reduce anxiety and increase people's confidence. I would get up and make my daughter a high-protein power smoothie to take to school on big exam days.

When my brothers and I were little, our grade school had an annual Christmas assembly the week before the holiday break and all the classes had to perform. As a reward for singing loud and remembering most of our lines, we got to open a small present from under the tree and have hot cocoa before bed when we got home. It was a highly anticipated consequence every year. We could bank on it and it was so exciting.

Why You Care

As adults, it's becoming more and more common to get caught up in the tasks of our daily lives and completely lose touch with our bodies, our loved ones, and even our spiritual support system.

Eckhart Tolle says that most men live their lives in (what he calls) a chronic state of dysfunction, where chaos is our norm. Positive ritual breaks the patterns of chaos that drive us so deeply into the stress response. Recognizing that chaos in and of itself is not inherently bad. It's more how we respond to chaos that determines our state of mind.

Gaia and Eros

Think back to middle school Greek mythology. You may remember that chaos was described as the "original dark void," the condition from which all things were created. Notice I didn't say from which all *adversity* was created, but from which ALL things were created. If you recall, the first thing to come out of chaos was the deity, Gaia, aka Mother Earth (or Mother Nature). The second thing to come out of chaos was Eros, the God of Erotic Love (Yes, please). Here's what's cool about that: the two most basic derivatives of chaos are also the areas of our lives that have the greatest capacity for expansion and growth: Nature and Love.

NATURE is filled with examples of rituals we take for granted. The sun rises and sets every day, just like clockwork. You know that when the tide recedes that it will always return. Bears hibernate in the winter and birds mate in the Spring. Grass grows until it turns to seed and then it drops and grows more grass. At the macro level, the change of seasons is a perfect time for us to establish related rituals.

Bliss Break:

Most of us have a myriad of holiday traditions, but how many of you have small celebrations for the change of seasons? Small changes in your environment and personal habits can build anticipation and help shift gears into the next phase of the year. Try some of these or come up with your own:

- Trade your winter quilts for a white cotton duvet as the weather warms.
- Change out the drapes in your bedroom from heavy velvet to flowy linen.
- Grab a friend and go shopping for flowers and veggie plants on May Day and plant them together.
- Celebrate the summer solstice with an annual midnight dip in the pool.
- Honor every full moon with a group meditation.
- Share the excitement. In Kansas, we like to invite the neighbors over for a Sangria on the front porch during tornado warnings.
- Buy local. Our corner bagel shop premiers the pumpkin bagels on September 1st, so you can bet we're in line when they open.
- Vacation in town. City Market Sunday mornings are a favorite pastime during season.
- Invite a bunch of girlfriends or your kids pals over on New Year's Eve to make vision boards and ring in the new year with new intentions.
- Grow a garden, even if it's just herbs. There's nothing like harvesting from your own bounty.
- Weather changes are the perfect time to sort through your closet, bring seasonal clothes to the front and thrift anything you didn't wear the year before.
- In fact, purging of any kind is a very cathartic activity to ease the transition into the next quarter

Rain, Rain - Go Away

I was clipping along on my daily walk along the trails near my home. I got about two miles from the house when the sky began to darken with ominous clouds. It was threatening to intrude on my predictable routine and I remember feeling more than mildly irritated. Why is it, when we're kids, we run outside to play at the first sign of rain - the harder, the better! Then somewhere past that invisible line of maturity, the rain becomes something to protect ourselves from-not unlike love and intimacy.

At first, I couldn't feel the rain because the canopy of trees acted as a shelter. But as I relaxed into the sounds of the drops hitting the leaves, the thunder in the far distance and squirrels scurrying to get home, I felt an overwhelming desire to feel the rain on my face, to know how hard it was actually coming down. Then my logical mind began to work with me, for a change. I had to go home and shower anyway. It's not like I was trying to salvage a good hair day. By making a conscious shift in my perspective, I was able to look up to the sky in gratitude and be blessed by the cool summer refreshment after a hot, sweaty trek. Look for opportunities to create connections with the Earth. Being with nature is an almost forgotten pastime in our busy-ness.

Friends and Family

Ritual is about finding ways to intentionally create a more charmed life through deliberate, *repeatable* action. Nowhere is this more important than where we choose to exhibit love, both to others and to ourselves. Let's talk about others first, because this seems to come a little easier to the ladies than the self-care piece. Think back to when you were a kid. It's the things you did over and over again that you remember most clearly about growing up, isn't it? (Both the good and the bad.) Keep that in mind if you are raising children.

We had a giant forsythia bush in our front yard growing up. My dad told me it was called a "for Cynthia" and I had no idea other people had them until I was probably twelve years old.

Bliss Tip: Whether you have children or not, there are macro rituals that we create as a family, from where we spend every holiday to what religion or faith we share (or lack thereof). There are cultural habits that we inherit from our parents or guardians, and then there are tiny little norms that we create based on our personalities. By the way, a good ritual doesn't have to be meaningful, it just has to evoke a positive emotion. A private joke is a fabulous ritual that connects you with another person. Someone just says a word that sparks a memory and makes you laugh.

Brotherly Love

My brother and I used to dread Thanksgiving because we were forced to spend it with relatives we had very little in common with. So to provide ourselves with our own entertainment, we'd give each other some random or inappropriate word to somehow work into the conversation. I'll spare you most of the words because I would embarrass myself with my sophomoric humor, but it was usually some bodily function or eight-syllable word that you can't pronounce.

One year, he assigned me the word "erection." Concerned at first, I had a thought. I picked up a newspaper sitting on the coffee table and said, "Looks like the Mall of America is being built in Minneapolis. The erection date is May 15." It was a proud moment and he was visibly irritated. My work here was done. The word I gave him was "rectum." So, he says, "I used to have two Buicks, but I wrecked'em." I'm still pretty certain that was cheating, but I let him have it for creativity.

Vacation Rituals

I grew up in Missouri. Since we didn't have a lot of money growing up, all of our family vacations were a quick drive to the Ozarks, about three hours south. With a carload of kids, my parents got really creative with traveling rituals. We'd play the quarter game, which meant whoever could be quiet the longest got a quarter. I sucked at that game, but my youngest brother would usually get there with about $3 in spending money.

And along the vacation route, there are several places where they had to blast through rock to get the road through. So, there were signs everywhere that say, "Danger Falling Rock." My dad told us that Falling Rock was a native American Indian who died 100 years ago and still kept watch over tourists to keep them safe on their journey. We would spend hours looking for him.

It's the Little Things

You don't have to have a large family to foster traditions. It was just my daughter and me in our little house, so it was important to me that we build a sense of ritual to give her the feeling of a family unit. Predictability in our homes makes us feel safe and loved. Most of you have your morning routine, don't you?

My daughter had a very meticulous process she would go through for the tooth fairy every time. She would build a little tooth fairy condominium with her *Polly Pockets* furniture, complete with a workout facility and hot tub. After my girlie fell asleep, I would swap out the tooth and sprinkle glitter from her windowsill over to her bed and into the condo. When she woke up, I would act like I was annoyed, "Every time she comes, she makes the biggest mess and I have to clean it up!"

In fact, we had fairies for everything she was about to outgrow. We collected all the pacifiers in a basket and put them on the front porch one night for the binky fairy to take for the babies who still needed them in exchange for a big girl toy we found in the basket the next morning. I admit the bobbie (bottle) fairy didn't go as smoothly the first night, but you get the idea.

The Ties that Bind

Rituals open us up to opportunities to improve all our relationships. Never underestimate a regular "date night." Couples who proactively set aside time to invest in one another have a 60% higher chance of staying together because it shows commitment to the other person.

Bliss Tip: *Take turns planning the date and draw from themes, like Cultural, Educational, Physical, Spiritual, Adventure. If you draw Cultural, go to an art exhibit. If you draw Physical, do a bike tour, etc. Be creative.*

It's the little personal expectations that keep our friendships interesting, whether it's a yearly GF weekend to NYC to celebrate being cancer-free or a golf outing to celebrate your kids going back to school.

Every Mother's Day, my daughter and I would ask each other the question, "What's the one thing I could do for you (or quit doing that bothers you) that would make your life easier or improve our relationship?" So, instead of picking at each other for all the things that drive us crazy, we focus on one thing at a time, so it's doable. It's small things that we can commit to.

One time, I just asked her to get out of bed when I ask her to in the morning. Our mornings were frantic because we didn't have enough time. So that one thing would take a great deal of stress out of my life. She might ask me to set aside my work for ten minutes and give her my undivided attention when she gets home from school, just so she can tell me about her day. We both commit to doing that one thing consistently and soon it became how we operate with each other.

Every New Year's Eve, we do a burning bowl in the living room floor to release everything we don't want to take into the new year. I buy flash paper at the local magic shop so we don't burn down the house. Then after we make noise, toast, and kiss whoever's handy at midnight, we build vision boards together. It used to be just my daughter and me, but now we usually have a house full of friends and teenagers and we make a monster mess! It's pretty awesome!

Habits of Self-Care

Since the beginning of time, ritual has been used as a primary means of self-care. Our goal is to survey all our daily habits to make sure they are fostering *good* juju. If not, I challenge you to edit out those rituals that stress your body or they are because you feel bad after doing them: things like watching a news channel before you go to bed at night…or giving in to your carb craving every day at 2:00pm when your body is sure it needs a java chip frappucino to make it 'til 5:00.

Take the time to make a list of your rituals that no longer serve your greater vision for yourself, then replace them with "feel good" options. Spend ten minutes visioning before you close your eyes to sleep and get out of the office and take a walk when your body starts to drain. Soon, certain times of the day will trigger self-care as things to look forward to.

Love your work. If you don't love your work, create things in your environment and throughout your day to love. Bring in fresh flowers or a lamp from home to warm up your space. Lunch with someone who makes you laugh. Wear low maintenance clothes that fit well and make you feel powerful or beautiful.

Ritual is not mindless repetition. It's not doing things because our parents did it that way. Meaningful ritual creates positive emotional triggers that enhance your relationships and strengthen your connections.

BLISS BREAK - Create patterns of good feelings in ordinary tasks.

- Put together a playlist of upbeat songs specifically to clean the house to. Laundry is a lot more fun dancing to the beat of Bruno Mars.

- Make washing the dishes a more meditative time. Set an intention and visualize on it until the dishes are done. Buddhists call this practice "mindfulness." Wax on...wax off, right Mr. Miyagi?

- Once a week, take a different route to work or the store and observe the details around you.

- Become a tourist in your own city. Try restaurants, events, and live music you've never tried.

- We'd be shocked if we realized how often we judge other in our heads. When you're in public, find something about each person that you like. It could be their shirt or their smile or the way they show love to their child. Better yet, give them a compliment out loud.

- After you have received service from anyone (a cashier, waiter, ticket agent), send them some virtual love. I like to visualize glitter and hearts falling from the sky covering them with good juju. Do it every time, especially if they're rude. They need it the most.

Nurturing Your Spirit

You are made up of body, mind, and spirit. Neglecting any one of these areas can throw your world in a wobble. The term "spiritual practice" implies that you don't just believe in a higher power, but that we have created a mechanism for connecting to and leveraging that power. It doesn't have to be complicated or even time-consuming. You can reconnect with guidance outside yourself immediately, just by giving it your attention in the moment.

I've never been good at meditation unless it's guided, because I can't sit still and be quiet for that long. So, I do an active meditation during my daily walk through the wooded trails. It's there I get my best ideas and am able to disengage from the activities of my life. The spiritual journey is such a personal one and countless books have been written to support your growth. I wouldn't suggest what your practice should look like. I can only say from my experience how crucial it is to connect to something bigger than yourself. So much peace of mind comes from knowing you're not doing all this alone. There are no hard and fast rules for engagement here. Honoring any and all paths to spiritual bliss…just make sure you're on one of them.

They say bad habits are easier to acquire and harder to break. True bliss requires becoming conscious about the way we start and end our day. If our life is just a compilation of the thoughts we think and choices we make, then the things that show up most often become our legacy. Some rituals are intentional and some we've inherited. It may be time to take a non-judgmental inventory of our patterns and see which ones make us feel better and which ones diminish us. Just because you've always done it a certain way doesn't mean it serves you. Remember, adrenaline and anxiety come from the exact same endorphin. Watch people on a rollercoaster and see how it plays out. What brings one person exhilarating joy may send another person reeling into the fetal position. Happiness comes from honoring your personal boundaries and desires–and knowing yourself well enough to know what they are.

Chapter 12
Self-Love

Our deepest fear is not that we are inadequate.
Our deepest fear is that we are powerful beyond measure.
- Marianne Williamson, Author, Spiritual Leader and Politician

I've heard it said that when you're 20, you're so worried about what people think about you. Then when you're 40, you don't really care what people think of you. Finally, when you turn 60, you realize no one was really thinking of you at all. We could have saved ourselves years of anguish had we had this intel a little earlier in life. In our efforts to be seen as worthy in the eyes of everyone else, we spend years spinning cycles on stuff that adds absolutely no meaning or joy to our lives.

I don't mean to imply no one cares about you or ever thinks of you. Clearly, they do. But it was a very sobering and liberating day when I figured out, even though I have lots of fabulous people in my life who love me, they aren't sitting by their computer waiting for my next product to come out or assessing whether or not I'm having a bad hair day. Turns out, other people apparently have their own lives and haven't lost one moment of sleep over stuff that gets posted on my FB wall. Who knew? How much time and effort we waste trying to be who we think others want us to be. How others feel about us is minuscule compared to the impact of how we feel about ourselves.

Self-love is analogous to the foundation of a house. If the builder takes care, using durable, quality materials then the home will weather any storm. If he builds it out of cards, even a mild breeze will topple it. Loving who we are requires us to step outside ourselves at times so we can get a more accurate perspective of our flaws and capabilities.

A few things to consider for loving on YOU:

<u>Show Compassion</u>

In traditional Japanese culture, there's a world view centered around the acceptance of transience and imperfection. It's about seeing the perfection in the less than perfect. It's called wabi-sabi. If an object or expression can bring about a sense of serene melancholy and a spiritual longing within us, then that object could be said to be wabi-sabi. You've likely heard the concept of filling the pieces of broken pottery with gold. This is an invitation to pick up the broken pieces of your life, embrace your emotional scars, and transform your life with your new-found knowledge. Your scars are proof that despite life's hard knocks, you have emerged stronger and more beautiful.

Mistakes are not a sign of weakness. If you're not making mistakes every day, you're not trying hard enough. We tend to be forgiving of others as they navigate the nuances of life. It's time to be gentler with yourself on this learning journey. I've heard it said that "in order to get old and wise, first you have to be young and stupid!" I prefer the term ignorant, but I didn't write it.

Are you growing from your missteps or punishing yourself? Anyone who tells you they have it all figured out is blowing smoke up your pantaloons. If they're still in human form, they got some learnin' to do.

Bliss Tip: When you're tempted to berate yourself over some inherent flaw or flagrant error, ask yourself what you would do differently next time. If you have any kind of an answer, you've learned something and some good has come from it. Focus on learning.

Set Boundaries

We touched on this in the chapter on Tolerations, but I have some additional thoughts to add. You'll love yourself more fully when you set healthy limitations and say no to people, activities, and substances that deplete your energy or harm you physically. Some things you're very capable of doing well poorly express who you are, and you get to decline without having to explain yourself. Good boundaries are set to protect you – your time, your heart, your space, and your values.

Bring the right people into your life. A good barometer is to ask yourself how you feel after a couple of hours with someone. Do they give you energy or cause you to need a long nap? Just recently, I had to distance myself from someone who had been a dear friend for a number of years. You may notice, as you experience a higher level of success in your life, there will likely be people close to you who are unable to be supportive.

As you set a new intention for your life and begin to see progress, you become a mirror to others. Then they have a decision to make. They will either look at you and say, "I'll have what she's having" and take steps to keep up. Or, conversely, they'll see the reflection of what they should be doing-but aren't willing to do. Then they'll try to bring you back to where they are for their own comfort. Problem is, you can't un-know what you've grown to know.

Oscar Wilde claims, *"The mind once expanded can never regain its original shape."*

In my coaching practice, I see women pretend to not be enlightened to make others feel more comfortable. It never works. They know better now and that eventually exposes itself.

Finally, protect your time. It is your most precious asset. When I first meet with a client, I ask them what they value most in the world and they say all the right things: family, health, faith. Then I ask to see their calendar for the last six months. You can guess what I observe. There's virtually nothing on there to indicate any of those things are important to them. I don't want you to wake up five years from now and wonder what happened to the last five years of your life because it went to your To-Do list. Make sure your big-picture goals make it on that daily list. If you want to get a degree or lose fifty pounds or buy a house or take a trip to Peru or get regular massages, put something on your list every day in support of those things.

Bliss Tip: If one area of over-commitment is your job, you may not feel like you can say no to your boss. You don't have to. There are ways to set boundaries without actually saying no. If he/she approaches you with work you don't have time for, try one of these phrases:

- "I'm happy to do that. Based on what I have on my plate, it looks like I can get that to you by next Thursday. Is that okay?" Give yourself however much time is realistic. They may say next Thursday is fine or they may choose to do it themselves or ask someone else.

- "Of course, I can help you. Let's take a look at what I have pending and see what I can defer in order to prioritize this for you." This allows them to see your workload and make the decision about what to move to later. You haven't said no, but you haven't over-committed.

Take Care of Your Gorgeous Bod

When the To-Do list gets longer than a CVS receipt, one of the first things that falls off most women's radar is their physical self-care. It's honestly pretty amazing how long our bodies can keep plugging away with little or no attention given to it. And because it keeps getting up and going, we begin to think of it as just a vehicle for getting shit done. We all know the drill. We're supposed to eat right and exercise and drink eight glasses of water a day and get plenty of sleep. If you're waiting for the punch line…there isn't one, though I felt the collective eye roll as I was writing this.

Why is it people wait to start caring for their physical vessel after they've had a medical scare or lose a loved one unexpectedly? Yet on the scale of most important things to focus on, nothing ranks much higher than your health and well-being. When you don't have it, it's pretty pervasive.

An interesting piece of trivia for you: The word "priority" remained singular for 500 years after it was introduced into the English language. It wasn't considered plural until the 1900s. The U.S. is currently second only to Japan for stress-related death. In fact, it's so epidemic that Japanese insurance companies actually have an official name for *death by over-working*. It's called Karoshi and it accounts for thousands of deaths every year. But for many of us, our relentless pursuit of "doing" leads to less literal forms of death–everything from decline in our relationships to just our general motivation to drag our booty out of bed in the morning.

I'm not saying anything here you don't already know. My hope is that you'll see it in the context of creating more bliss in your life rather than just one more thing you have to add to that list. Our natural instinct is to go for the low-hanging fruit on our To-Do list because there's an actual endorphin that's released when we check something off. It feels good to do the menial stuff first because we feel like we're accomplishing more. In fact, how many times have you thought about something you did earlier in the day and you add that to your list just so you can cross it off? I know I'm not the only one who does that. Anyway, the point is you may be completing lots of tasks but not really accomplishing much that has any real impact on your life. That's the hamster wheel syndrome.

Prioritize your beautiful body. Whatever state of neglect it may be in is not its fault, so don't criticize it. It keeps showing up for you and asks so little in return. Think of it as a small child who's been ignored. She may be unruly or dishevelled, and she might embarrass you at times, but you wouldn't beat up on the child. You would love her and teach her and comfort her in healthy ways. Your body is the gift that keeps on giving and deserves to be cared for lovingly.

Bliss Tip: Go back to your Joy List from Chapter 2 and pick one thing to do for yourself every day.

Build Self-Efficacy

One of the key strengths of resilience is the belief we are capable of solving problems as they arise and faith in our ability to succeed. It's like the *Little Engine That Could*, "I think I can. I think I can." It doesn't mean you always have the answers. It means you have the confidence that you can figure it out or seek out a resource to help. Referring back to the Serenity Prayer:

> "…and the wisdom to know the difference"

We expend entirely too much energy on the stuff we have absolutely no control over and wonder why we feel stuck and less competent. Becoming aware of the values that drive you and seeking alignment between them and the decisions you make for yourself will go a long way toward trusting your instincts. Celebrate the small wins when things turn out the way you planned. There's nothing like success for boosting self-confidence. Keep a bottle of champagne chilled in the fridge just in case a friend announces their promotion, or you get a kick-ass haircut or just because it's Tuesday and you haven't killed anyone at work yet. I high-five myself when I make all the way to the top of the stairs to my home office without splashing coffee on the carpet. It's a special skill.

The only way to get better at anything is to do it. Then screw it up. Then try it again with new information. I was driving home from a New Year's Eve party a few years ago and passed a lighted marquee on the front of a church. The sign read, "May you only make NEW mistakes in the 2018." 'Nuff said.

Bliss Tip: When you set a goal to accomplish something, seek out an accountability partner. This should be someone you trust to be both supportive and honest. Give them permission to check on your progress and call you on your excuses. Use them to pow-wow ideas and process your mistakes. If you tend to be self-critical, having a second perspective will help you see how far you've come.

Show Up as Your Best Friend

Let's get real…would you let anyone talk to you the way you talk to yourself? Moreover, would you talk to anyone else the way you talk to yourself? Of course, you wouldn't - or you wouldn't have any friends. One of my favorite TV ads was a Dove commercial released in France a few years ago. They gave several women a journal and had them write down all their negative self-talk for a period of time and then turn the notebooks in. Dove turned their journal words into a dialog between two actresses and invited the original women back one at a time for a coffee at a local shop.

The actresses were sitting at the next table and one was saying the critical words to the other at the table, so the woman could overhear their conversation. To say they were shocked would be an understatement. It was enough to help each of them recognize how violent their self-criticism had been. It's very touching to watch. Google it on *YouTube* (Dove Commercial Self Talk). The point clearly made: if it's not acceptable to say to someone else, why would you say it to yourself?

No one except you, goes to bed with you and wakes up with you every single day of your life. You know what makes you laugh and what makes you cry. You know what excites you and what scares you and what gives you comfort. So, who better to be your best friend than YOU. Learn to enjoy your own company.

Bliss Tip: Most of us have a filter in our head that keeps us from verbalizing everything that runs through our thoughts. So, even as we might think an unkind thought about another, we have a mechanism for making sure we don't say it out loud. If you've been unconsciously spewing negative self-talk for a while, it's gonna' take some practice. A way to minimize the scolding is to use that filter to at least make sure you don't criticize yourself out loud to yourself and others. This includes self-effacing jokes. Your subconscious doesn't register that you're joking. As you become more affirming verbally, your inner dialog will start to get the message.

It's the Little Things

Finally, think of all the small things you do for others and do them for *you*, too. Something as simple as firing up the waffle iron for one waffle or grabbing fresh flowers for your desk sends a distinct message of worthiness to your soul. I used to think making my bed was a fruitless task. Nobody saw it and I was just going to get right back in it. One day, I took an assessment that gauged how much time I invested in self-care. One question was whether I made my bed every day. Then we were asked to pick one thing we didn't check and start doing it for ourselves. I chose making my bed because it was easy and didn't cost anything. It was the low-hanging fruit. The next day, I got up and dressed, pulled up the blankets and tossed all the pretty pillows in place, went to work and forgot about it. When I got home and walked into my bedroom, I was overcome with the most overwhelming feeling of caring. It was like housekeeping had been there and I felt so loved. From then on, I always make my bed. Self-love is the beginning of a life-long romance. You are the most important relationship you'll ever have. You are the center of your Universe. Never forget that.

Chapter 13
Contentment

*If I ever go looking for my heart's desire again, I won't look any further than my own back yard. Because if it isn't there,
I never really lost it to begin with.*
— Dorothy, lead Character from <u>The Wizard of Oz</u>

Because I make my living by helping people get from where they are to where they want to go, I find it hard sometimes to get out of self-improvement mode. Anyone else relate to that? Shoot, this book will likely end up on the shelves of the *Self Improvement* genre. I believe we're here on this physical plane to learn and experience and grow. That said, reaching for the next stage of competency on a continuous basis takes us out of the present moment which is not conducive to bliss. If you're always reaching for your next level, you forget to bask in the beauty and awareness of where you are right now.

<u>The Addiction of Up Leveling</u>

I was making plans to do a business trip to New England last year. I always try to schedule a few extra days up there to spend with my buds. I was talking to the friend I was planning to stay with in Massachusetts. She is the poster child for up-leveling your life and I always leave there inspired to play bigger. That's one of the reasons we connect. I was talking to her prior to my visit and she asked, "What do you want to do while you're up here? We can hit the gym every day and work up a new routine for you." Without thinking, I said, "Sure." Then after I hung up the phone, I clearly recognized that I really had no desire to do that at all. I mean I did, but not that weekend.

What I was really thinking is *I only have four days in one of the most beautiful places in the country I really don't want to spend it inside a building smelling dirty sweat socks and facing the scale. I can do that when I get back home.* For a few minutes, I felt a little guilty about that. But that nano-second of getting real with myself made me wonder if, as a generation, do we even know how to approach life *not* in self-improvement mode?

As an experiment, I decided to try something really scandalous on that trip. I set a goal that, for the entire time I was there, I was not going to try to improve myself in any way. I didn't buy any miracle potions. I didn't go to the gym. I didn't read any Deepak Chopra. I didn't even wash my hair the whole weekend. The message isn't to quit taking care of yourself. It's all about balance. The point is: while it's our nature to grow and expand, sometimes enhancing the human spirit comes when we quit trying to fix ourselves. I'm here to remind you that not only are you not broken, you're not alone.

<u>Contentment is a Dying Art</u>

If even just for the day, grant yourself permission to simply be still–to listen to what your body wants to eat and let the car turn wherever it feels inspired to go. Allow your mind to ponder really useless questions like what petroleum product they use to make that stuff in the bottom of boba tea or whether you prefer Khloe Kardashian as a blond or a brunette. (I'm still undecided. I think she looks smokin' either way). Perhaps just for a weekend, you don't need to save anybody or be more productive.

I invite you to join me in doing absolutely nothing to improve yourself today. Give yourself a much-needed break from all the *doing* and just *be*. You are a glorious Spirit with skin on. At a Soul level, you know you're complete. Feel the sweet contentment that comes from already being magnificent!

Bliss Tip: I invite you to stop reading for just a minute and look around you. How many things can you notice that you're truly quite content with? What do you observe or remember that you wouldn't change a thing about it? Example: I love my office layout. I kept moving stuff around until it worked for me. I could always use more space, but being in here makes me feel good, so I focus on that for a minute. Also, it took me way too long to finish this book. I could beat myself up for that, but I'm finding a sense of accomplishment for just staying with it. And that makes me feel good, so I focus on that for a minute. It is enough.

Acceptance is Key

Please don't confuse contentment with complacency. Complacency is followed by a sense of low-grade regret or neutrality of any real emotion. Contentment is better equated to peace of mind. It's the knowing you *can* and *will* continue to grow, but there's no sense of urgency. There's no guilt or obligation. It's an inherent understanding that you're living life on your terms according to your timeline. Nothing provides you with more relief than your genuine acceptance of how things are right now.

A minister friend used to have a radio show where people could call in and ask him questions. I was listening in once when a caller asked him how she was supposed to accept that her life was prosperous when her bills were piling up and she was afraid to even open them for fear they were more than she could manage. I think we've all been at that place of paralysis in some area of our lives, so you know how that feels. He told her to open her bills, figure out where she stood, and make payment arrangements first.

Sweeping them under the rug was putting her in a place of denial, so she couldn't move past it. The second half of his message was "You need to know the *Truth* but manage the *facts*." The capital "T" Truth is that everything is figure-outable. But knowing and accepting her current state was the first step to getting out of it. It's like waiting for the doctor to deliver the results of your blood work. The greatest fear is in the not knowing. Once you have some clarity, then you can exhale and make better decisions.

What Is It You Really Want?

I'm on the Board for an organization called the Women's Employment Network. They have an amazing program for helping women build the skills and confidence to financially support themselves and their families. They'll learn tons of tactical technical skills, but I want them to be really clear what their motivation is before they step into this program, so they stick with it. A typical conversation goes like this:

Me: Why are you interested in this program?
Them: Because I need a job.
Me: Why do you need a job?
Them: To have money.
Me: Why do you need money?
Them: To pay my bills.
Me: Why do you need to pay your bills? (Admittedly, they're starting to get pretty annoyed at this point)
Them: So, I can have a place to live.
Me: Why do you need a place to live?
Them: So, my kids can have a safe yard to play in and I can feel like I'm finally home…

NOW, we're getting somewhere!

In the pursuit of happiness, sometimes we forget it's not somewhere else. You don't need to do anything or go anywhere to know bliss. Most people think they are seeking a thing or a job or a partner, but we're really only looking for one thing. Everything we desire is ultimately because we think it will make us happier. I see this over and over again in my work. Women call me because they want a promotion or a relationship or more success. Then when they get those things, they're still unfulfilled. You've heard the stories of people who won the lottery. The added funds just made them more of what they already were. If you've historically focused on what's wrong with your life, you'll just buy things that are high maintenance, more work, and have more things to worry about.

Being okay with where we are is counter to what we've been taught, especially as strong women. We've been socialized that we have to work harder than our male counterparts to break even. And frankly, some of us really enjoy the process of being a better version of ourselves every year. I'm never one to squelch the fun and sense of accomplishment you get from growth. From a place of acceptance, rather than wanting change because you think you're lacking in some way, let self-love and gratitude inspire any transformation you choose to invest in.

Chapter 14
Gratitude in Times of Chaos

For everyone who helped me start
And for everything that broke my heart
For every breath, for every day of living
This is my Thanksgiving.
- Don Henley, Lyricist and Drummer for The Eagles

This one may seem like a big "Duh," but I'm not just talking about giving thanks for what you have. That's a given. I'm talking about seeing the good in all situations and things and people. Finding love in the stuff that doesn't feel as good is more challenging and crucial for discovering consistent peace. In the midst of our daily chaos, life can sometimes feel out of control and it's tough to see past the facts in front of our face.

Consider the butterfly in the chrysalis. The structure of the caterpillar has to completely dissolve into this gelatinous mass during the pupal stage in order for the new insect to form. Our own personal transformations are not unlike that. I like to call this "living in the goo." Now, that doesn't mean your whole life has to fall apart in order for you to grow. The butterfly transformation doesn't happen all at once. The metamorphosis is gradual and very deliberate. Most of us struggle with the ambiguity of living in the goo because we can't always see the beauty that's about to emerge from it.
A friend of mine likes to say,

"When one door closes, another one opens -
             but it's hell in the hallway!"

Dancing with Chaos

I'm here to challenge your thinking about the chaos in your life. I looked up the word *chaos* in my online Webster's and found the disparity between the two definitions to be fascinating.
Here's what it said:

1. A state of utter confusion in a given situation.

    Okay…that's fully what I expected it to say. But check out the second description…

2. The confused state of primordial matter before the creation of distinct forms.

    Hmmmm, that's interesting. In essence, this is saying chaos is simply all the information in a given scenario is in front of you- in no particular order- and you get to decide what you're going to glean from it. You get to determine what it all means to you. You see, nothing comes to us already in order. That's what separates us from most other animals – opposable thumbs for texting and the ability to make reason out of the madness. It's called free will and so many of us forget we have it when the proverbial crapola hits the fan.

    As if free will itself isn't enough to be thankful for, we get the opportunity to determine at any given moment what we want to manifest into our experience. The contrast of "good" and "bad" experiences is important because you can't know what you truly want in your life until you've clearly observed what it is you don't want. It's impossible to have clarity around your greatest desires without observing both perspectives. For this, we must be grateful.

We all have our Phoenix-from-the-ashes stories, don't we? It's not about trying to scrap some good out of the adversity; it's about re-framing our perspective to see the perceived adversity as merely a data-point, a snapshot in time, a reflection of past thinking that brings us into awareness so we can think a new thought.

Let's break it down a little further because most chaos falls into three general categories:

External Chaos

This may include global issues, things you see on the news or any other circumstance you just *happen* to find yourself in where you feel you have done nothing or little to contribute to its creation.

In Robert Brumet's book, *Birthing a Greater Reality*, he talks about "the Butterfly Effect" - also known as the *Chaos Theory*. Essentially, it has been proven that, because weather patterns are such chaotic systems, their predictability is dependent upon extreme accuracy in recording conditions like temperature, barometric pressure, wind velocity, etc. Weather prediction is so sensitive that, hypothetically, if we had perfect measurements from every point on earth, but we missed a butterfly flapping its wings in China, then an unpredicted storm could occur in New York City and alter the course of the global forecast! Is that not crazy?

The theory shows that there is a hidden order of the universe and as we are willing to dance with chaos in our lives, we open the door to personal transformation happening in ways that we could have never predicted!

BLISS BREAK:

One of my favorite practices when I feel like my world is coming down on me, and everything's out of control, I learned from Abraham-Hicks. While they recommend this activity for when you're generally in a pretty positive headspace, I find it useful when I'm struggling to find an obvious reason to be happy in a given moment.

Try doing a "**Rampage of Appreciation.**" You start by looking around your current environment and find something that pleases you. It could be the fabric of the shirt someone is wearing or the yellow house on the corner or a favorite plant – anything, really. Then just focus your attention on it until you get a pleasant feeling. Look around and find something else to appreciate. Then another...and so on. Some days, you may just be grateful for the heat in your home or your kid took a nap or that someone else cleaned out the kitty litter. There are always dozens of things around you to appreciate if you're actively looking for them.

Then you're just going to move through your day finding things you appreciate. I promise you, it makes it impossible to stay in a state of fear or worry for long. You are literally shifting your energy to a more positive vibration, which means you'll be attracting more and more things to be grateful for. Just try it. It seriously works.

Iceberg Chaos

I use this analogy to identify the kind of chaos that shows up over and over again in your life. I call them icebergs because the nature of the iceberg is that it is deeply rooted and so much bigger than you can see on the surface. We are creating habitual chaos based on our core, underlying beliefs about how the world operates.

They say that insanity is defined by doing the same things over and over and expecting a different result. Chaos often shows itself as repetitive stress patterns that the less enlightened like to call "a run of bad luck." But it's long been proven how critical our beliefs are in shaping the world around us.

True Sin

Eckhart Tolle says, "true sin is to live unskillfully, blindly, trapped in our habitual patterns of thinking, thus causing ourselves and others to suffer unnecessarily."

Dr. Andrew Shatte, author of *The Resilience Factor*, calls this *catastrophizing*...where we take a fairly simple and non-threatening thought and spiral quickly to the internal chaos that skews our perception of the threat and the solution.

Einstein's theory of a friendly Universe plays into this equation- because there is no absolute outcome to any situation. We were taught in school that or every action there's a reaction, meaning that when Adversity strikes, it has a Consequence (A=C). But Dr. Shatte tells us that's only half of the equation because two people can have the exact same adversity happen to them and have completely different outcomes.

In study after study, science has disclosed that what you believe about what's happening is the number one determining factor in how it turns out. So, instead of A=C (Adversity=Consequence), it would more accurately be stated that A+B=C (<u>A</u>dversity + your <u>B</u>elief about what caused it and what's possible = the actual <u>C</u>onsequence). We see this play out all the time. When something unfavorable happens, how well you recover depends on:

1. Why you think it happened
2. How capable you think you are
3. What you believe the impact is
4. How emotionally attached you are
5. Whether or not you can see a solution
6. Whether you believe it's your fault or someone else's

So many things factor into how the adversity ends and—sans all the information—your subconscious takes shortcuts based on your belief system. That's cool if your beliefs support your success. But if you have a negatively skewed perception of yourself and those old tapes are playing in your head, you may be dead ended at problem-solving. In a nutshell, the results of your life are 10% what happens to you and 90% what you believe about it.

So, we have to examine the chaos in our lives to discern how much of it is self-inflicted. You can remove the largest degree of chaos from your life simply by thinking a new thought.

Bliss Tip: *The only way to eliminate a negative belief is to replace it with another belief. Seek out evidence that supports that new belief and start telling that story. For a while, you may have to write out the new thoughts or affirmations and carry them with you. Throughout the day, pull out your notes and read them aloud. Use these replacement thoughts every time you're tempted to relay that old belief until you shift the self-sabotaging pattern.*

Intentional Chaos

This is the *undoing* of the status quo on purpose. It's where you proactively shake stuff up with the intent to create something better than what currently exists. It's the caterpillar in the chrysalis.

Normally, when we think of resilience, our thoughts go to stories of overcoming adversity, staying calm under pressure or navigating through day-to-day obstacles. It is those things, but one component of resilience that is commonly overlooked is the proactive capacity for reaching out to others or instigating change simply for the purpose of enhancing your life. This is the pinnacle of utilizing chaos in your favor! Though, in my experience as a Coach and a Mentor, I can tell you there are very few people who actually do it. The reason being, most of us are so resistant to change, because it traditionally is something that we are responding *to*, not *seeking* out. The general perception of change is that it is usually stressful and rarely in my best interest. So, to shake things up intentionally feels counter intuitive. It's not natural. Actually, it's completely natural, but we're scared to death of it. What if whatever I find is worse than what I have? What if I have to lose something important to me in order to get there? What if I fail? What if I get hurt?

I want you to think about the massive changes that have already happened throughout your life. Honor the shifts that have taken place that required you to show up in radically new ways. What you have already accomplished is quantum and you have proven to yourself you were up to the challenge. Change is rarely easy and not always pretty. But what we know for sure is that you're in transformation whether you're in charge of the process or not. As soon as you think you have it all figured out and you can bask in the monotony of your existence, something will happen to remind you that energy must move. The key here is to be a step ahead of the curve. Instead of waiting for life to happen to you, you get to decide what you want to experience and take steps to maximize the chances of getting there.

We can learn a lot from the mother eagle by how she teaches her babies to fly. Eagles tend to perch very high off the ground, so it's a terrifying prospect for a tiny baby eagle, still insecure, having never flown, to throw its body fearlessly off a treacherous cliff. So, the mama has to have a system for getting them to venture out when it's time. As she builds her nest prior to laying eggs, she'll line the nest with thorns and bristle and then pad it on top with cotton and grasses to protect the eggs. But as the babies begin to outgrow the nest, they may show no signs of attempting to fly. When the time is right, the mother eagle will begin, a little each day, pulling the padding out of the nest. Soon, all that remains are the thorns and sticks. Eventually, it becomes more painful for the babies to stay in the nest than it is to make the leap. While that may sound a little sadistic, what the mama eagle knows is if those babies don't fly, they'll die there.

Too often, we are the baby birds and aren't willing to create the chaos necessary for the evolution of our growth until it's so painful that we *have* to do something. And it's difficult to have clarity in our objectives when we are in survival mode.

Our cultural bias is that chaos is bad, that something is wrong. Chaos means we are somehow out of control, which is not valued in our culture. Chaos frightens the ego. When we realize that having control over anything is a complete illusion, we lose our fear of chaos.

You are not here to live a life of mediocrity.
You're definitely not here to play small.
Francis Ford Coppola once said,

"Anything you do with intense passion invites chaos."
With that said…let the dance begin!

Chapter 15
Your New Story

I'm writing my story so that others may see fragments of themselves.
- Lena Waithe, American Screenwriter and Producer

"When you were born, you were given a spark of life. This spark vitalizes you until your life here ends. In between, your role is to use that human spirit to express yourself and contribute to your community." This is a quote from one of my favorite movies of all time, *Phenomenon,* with John Travolta. He played a character by the name of George Malley. His story emphasizes the power of human capacity. And his quote reminds us that ordinary people possess extraordinary potential. But here's where we get snagged. We're waiting until we feel completely *ready* or believe we're worthy of expressing what's in our hearts. We're worried that our ideas aren't quite gelled enough, well-thought-out enough, sufficiently validated for human consumption. Heaven forbid we make ourselves vulnerable by exposing our silly opinions and innermost dreams to the risk of criticism–worse yet, failure.

Truth is, if we all waited until we had our total you-know-what together, nothing would ever get invented and powerful inspiration may never happen. Some of us have hesitated to express our opinion or live out loud for risk of being seen as aggressive or "too much". This self-doubt has been propagated by some as the residual effect of gaslighting or lack of positive reinforcement when we've tried to be seen before. But I'm here to remind you that **you are allowed to be both a masterpiece and a work in progress, simultaneously**. And it's time to give yourself permission to tell the story of the YOU you've come here to be.

Alan Fine of Inside Out Coaching reminds us, "It's not that people don't *know* how to act. They just don't *act* on what they know." So, if we think we know what we want our life to be like, why aren't we doing those things? We've talked a lot about interference and distraction. That certainly plays a part. But the most impactful tool for shaping your reality is the story you continue to propagate over and over about who you are. I'm not just talking about the things you *say*. Remember the action piece in the manifestation cycle? What you believe and talk about all the time determines what actions you take (or don't take). In this chapter, you not only get to reframe your language, you're going to make sure your actions are aligned, so you can see some movement in the right direction. While it's monumentally important to shift your thinking and words first, the tangible effects happen when you start doing something different than you were doing before.

Your Internal GPS

I invite you now to take a closer look at the expectations you've set for yourself with your old story. I promised not to leave you hanging with your old, destructive self-talk. As a reminder, your historical patterns needn't sadden you–or define you. How you got there or why you did it doesn't matter. Try not to enter into the meaning you've given it. Your old story is just a data point. Think of your evolution like the navigation system in your car. When you get into your car and seek directions, your GPS only needs to know one thing — "where do you want to go?" At no juncture will it ask you "where were you before that' or "why you stayed there so long?" It doesn't care because it's not germane to where you're going.

Part of my resilience training taught me to question my thinking when I was going down a rabbit hole of negativity. My high school debate was good preparation for challenging myself, too. During a debate tournament, you never knew which side of a topic you were going to have to support, so it taught me the value of seeing both sides of an issue. I was grateful for both of these experiences at three o'clock in the morning one day shortly after I split with my daughter's dad. I recall waking abruptly and sitting straight up in bed. My mind was racing with self-doubt and fear of the future. Questions rapid-fired through my head: *What if I can't raise a child by myself? What if I can't financially support her? What if I'm not a good mom?* It was irrational and terrifying, as are most thoughts at three a.m.

In my soul, I knew all those thoughts were bull, but they still felt very real in the moment. The next step in the recovery process here is for you to search for **real evidence** that's counter to what you're telling yourself. Now, it wouldn't have been helpful to just say to myself, "You're a good mom." I needed real data. So, one at a time, I had to recall some proof. I reminded myself of people far less equipped to raise children (teen parents) who produced happy, healthy kids. The facts were that I had never been truly unemployed, and if I were, I had a number of marketable skills. And I went through a laundry list of things I was doing right with her. Eventually I had enough evidence and could go back to sleep.

What I also learned is resilience isn't just about optimism ("I'm good enough, I'm smart enough, and gosh darn it, people like me" – Stuart Smalley, Saturday Night Live circa 2014). Resilience is more about accuracy. As you work through this next activity, avoid just saying the opposite of the negative thought. Search for real evidence—in your own life or someone else's—that proves the other side of the story.

BLISS BREAK: Step 1 of 3

Practice challenging your own thinking by re-framing a questionable belief or expectation you've been carrying around for way too long. Here's your chance to cross-examine your self-doubt and disprove the lies it propagates.

In the left column, you're going to pull some items from your Old Story in Chapter 3—things you commonly say to yourself about each topic that don't support your happiness. Then in the right column, you're going to search for *real* evidence that's counter to each statement. This isn't just a more positive statement; it's real, tangible evidence. Be a journalist. Again, use your bliss journal if you need more space.

Examples:

Old Story	Counter Evidence
I'll never be able to make good money without a degree.	A third of the world's millionaires only have a high school diploma.
	I have an entrepreneurial spirit and there's a myriad of ways to educate myself these days.
I've never had kids. I'm going to be a terrible mom.	When my sister had her first child, she was clueless and scared to death, but she figured it out and she's a great mom.
	I have family and a great support system close by that I can count on to help me.

Old Story about MY BODY	Counter Evidence

Old Story about MY FINANCES	Counter Evidence

Old Story about MY RELATIONSHIPS	Counter Evidence

Old Story about MY SELF WORTH	Counter Evidence

A Glance into the Future

Telling a new story may feel a little awkward at first and it takes practice to replace the story you've been telling for years. But now that you can prove that stuff wasn't true after all, it becomes unnecessary to drudge that old garbage up anymore. This frees you up to create the life you want without the heavy baggage. A lighter load frees up all kinds of energy and space for the level of bliss you deserve. This next part of your journey is where you get super clear about what you want to be experiencing more of every day. Grab your journal and a cup of chamomile tea with a cinnamon stick, find a quiet spot to hunker down and give yourself at least an hour to really connect with your vision.

BLISS BREAK: Step 2 of 3

Here's where you get to write a shiny new life script. It's now time to start creating a picture of the life you desire (and know is possible for you). Use the data you've gleaned from your old story to inform the lifestyle and circumstances that you're going to create. Just write it in story form and use as much space in your journal as it takes for you to feel complete.

Your Mission:
Assume you run into a friend a year from today whom you haven't seen at all in the past year. You invite them to grab a beverage and catch up. They ask you what's going on in your life and you're going to describe your life to them, in vivid detail, as if everything were exactly the way you would want it to be.

Describe your career, your relationships, your health, your home, your hobbies, your faith, your clothes, your vacations...
Talk about every area of your life. Your friend has all the time in the world to listen and is thrilled for you!

<u>Here are the only guidelines:</u>

- This will be titled simply *My New Story*.

- Write it in present tense, as if you were telling about your life, in the moment, a year from now.

- Use as much detail as you can envision. Include all your senses: sounds, smells, colors, flavors, specific people and places.

- Avoid double negatives (i.e., getting out of debt or losing weight). Instead you would say something like "financially secure" or "fit, healthy body."

- Have FUN with this-the sky's the limit.

Congratulations on making the commitment to get clear about your goals and dreams. Edwene Gaines, author of *The Four Spiritual Laws of Prosperity*, claims we give Amazon more attention that we do the Universe. You would never send Amazon a note and say, "Just send me whatever you think I'd like." So, how can you expect the stars to align for you if you don't really know what you desire? Until you get a distinct picture of what you want to create in your life, the chances of getting there are slim to none. Now that you've claimed your vision, keep it actively in front of you. Read it often. Create a vision board of pictures and affirmations to support it. Most importantly, you must live as if it were already so. Do this and watch the right people and resources show up in your life almost magically.

<u>*They Will Find You*</u>

I'm in the business of supporting women and helping them transform their lives. I knew early on I wanted to start providing weekend retreats as a part of my offerings. I've seen the power of women coming together, away from their daily lives, for the purpose of renewal and insight. In my early days of building my Bliss Camps, a friend of mine mailed me a physical article from a magazine about a woman who was doing something similar very successfully in California. The name of her property was *Campowerment* and I was mesmerized by her story. I carried this article in my laptop case for weeks and re-read it several times. One morning on a short flight from Kansas City to Atlanta, I had the rare treat of having no one sit in the middle seat of my row. That virtually never happens. I'm a window girl. A well-dressed woman about my age joined me on the aisle. It was a quiet flight and I noticed she was typing feverishly on her phone the entire time. It honestly looked like she was writing a novel and I was impressed by how skillfully she navigated the tiny keyboard.

We landed early, so our gate wasn't available. For the first time, she spoke, and I asked her if she was writing a book. She explained that she was correcting an article written by a columnist for the NY Times about her business and it was due this afternoon. I asked her the name of her business. (You know where this is going, right?) She said her name was Tammi and she owned a place on the west coast called *Campowerment*. Seriously, what are the odds? My first thought was dismay that she'd been sitting next to me the whole time and we didn't talk. I was also a little embarrassed that I spent the whole flight trying to scrape off my remaining gel polish, like a dork. But mostly I just took it as a sign that the Universe is definitely paying attention, whether we are or not.

Search for Contradictions

The final piece required for setting yourself up for the life you've just claimed is making sure you aren't blatantly or accidentally doing the opposite of what you say you want. You're now going to search for contradictions–things you may be doing that blocks your best efforts. I had a client who hired me to help her find a life partner. One day, we had plans to attend an event together and her car battery was dead, so I offered to pick her up. When I arrived at her home, the garage door was up. While she had a two-car garage bay, she had parked right square in the middle and had boxes piled on either side. I had a thought and asked her if I could take a peek in her closet. She looked perplexed but agreed. Aha! Just as I suspected. There wasn't room to wedge another t-shirt into that closet. She wasn't a messy person, but she had managed to fill every vacant space in the house by herself. You see, though she was *saying* she wanted a partner to join her in her home, her actions were sending a very different message. There was literally nowhere for another person to be. Her obvious action was to make some space. Clean out a drawer in the bathroom and buy an extra toothbrush, for heaven's sake.

Now it's your turn…

BLISS BREAK: Step 3 of 3

Using the new story you just wrote, write each vision you have for your life in a separate square in the left column. (Copy these columns into your journal for maximum space). Now you're ready to search your environment. Also pay attention to your words to gently notice where you may be verbally contradicting what you say you want. It's fun and enlightening when you find them. Channel your inner Nancy Drew. Then determine an action you can take to be better aligned with your vision.

VISION	CONTRADICTION	ACTION

It All Adds Up

It's not likely going to be the quantum goals you set for yourself that will be creating the new, improved you. It's the little ways you shift your language or appreciate things around you that will reap the greatest benefits. Don't get me wrong, I'm all about thinking big and in no way mean to discourage your BHAG (Big Hairy Audacious Goals). It's entirely possible to look like Christie Brinkley by swimsuit season or clean 38 years of clutter out of your garage next weekend. People have done it. Hold that thought if it makes you feel good and inspires you.

Might I suggest that you allow yourself to find renewal in just setting positive *intentions* for your life and just start *being* that person…one small change at a time. But mostly, bliss will come not so much from what you add to your life, but what you are willing to leave in the past. Lighten your load by releasing whatever no longer serves you (people, habits, things).

What Would This Woman Do?

At the end of the day, this is the most important question you can ask yourself. If you keep your one-year vision in front of you and use it as a compass for decision-making, you will see miraculous shifts in your life. If every time you get ready to do something, you look at your vision and ask: Would the woman I wrote about do *this*? Would she eat this? Would she live here? Would she hang out with this person? Would she spend money on that thing? If the answer is "no," then you know you're about to engage in something that is moving you further from the life you want. If the answer is "yes," proceed with great joy.

Chapter 16
Everything Is a Miracle - or Nothing Is

Miracles happen every day. Change your perception of what a miracle is and you'll see them all around you.
- Jon Bon Jovi, Front Man for the Rock Band, Bon Jovi

My man, Albert Einstein, always said it best: "There are only two ways to live your life—as though nothing is a **miracle**, or as though **everything is a miracle**." If you can get past the trite, cross-stitch pillow sentimentality of this statement and dig a little deeper; if you can learn to expect greater happiness more often than not; if you make an effort to assume more positive intent from others, then you'll start to see more true evidence of bliss in your everyday moments.

<u>How Does It Make You Feel?</u>

I've never been particularly attached to my belongings. In fact, not unlike many of you, I too have historically fallen prey to the notion that material wealth somehow separates us from a spiritual connection. Fortunately, a little well-earned life experience has allowed me to release that misnomer, but still there's very little that I can't live without (excluding my weighted blanket and life-size Mike Rowe cardboard cut-out). Maturity has granted me the serenity to accept the things that bring me joy, courage to scrap the things that don't and the wisdom to know the difference! (Or something like that...)

So, what criteria can you use to determine whether or not something (or some*one*) is a keeper? Intrinsic value does not determine worth. The first step is to assess how this person, place, or thing makes you *feel*...

I was wandering through a discount clothing store with my daughter a while ago. I was merely an observer while she selected some things to try on. At the risk of sounding like a martyr, I rarely felt the need to shop for myself when I was raising a kid. And I wasn't that day. But something caught my eye. I walked past it several times, attempting to ignore it, but some invisible vortex kept pulling me closer. I was being seduced by an inanimate object and I was resisting with the conviction of a stubborn toddler. But then I touched it… and it was all over! The feel of cashmere between my fingers – and it was powder pink, my favorite color. Then I looked at the price tag and almost swallowed my gum. "Are you kidding me? An $80 scarf at Marshall's? What kind of a lunatic would pay that? I'm not gonna' buy it. I'm just gonna' put it on for a second."

When I wrapped this scarf around my neck and nuzzled my face into its luxurious softness, the strangest thing happened — I began to cry. Totally unprovoked, huge tears started rolling down my cheeks. Passersby looked at me like I was a freak and I knew that scarf was going home with me. I'm still not entirely sure what inspired such an emotional reaction. But what I suspect, in that moment, wrapped in luxury and the texture of the Gods, I felt *cared for*. So often, we focus our energies on making sure that all those around us have their needs met. Allowing myself to have this *thing* was not about shopping for myself. Saying "yes" to this scarf represented a warm, soft hug of pure unapologetic success. I give away a lot of myself and I deserved it. And so, my Dear, do you.

As you wander through your own environment, do a check-in of the stuff and people you have around you. Allow yourself the freedom of releasing the things that don't inspire a positive emotional reaction. Listen carefully and you can hear the sound of everything that doesn't matter disappear.

Cultivate a "Blissipline"

This is my favorite new term, dubbed by Dr. Michael Bernard Beckwith, minister at Agape Spiritual Center in Beverly Hills. The concept implies bliss as a practice. It reminds us bliss isn't something you have to seek out; it's around you all the time. Being awake to the awesome that exists within eye or ear shot at any given moment—and choosing to see it—is the secret happy people know. The reason I had you create your Joy List early on is so you can be reminded of how much beauty and fun is already out there for the taking.

There are times in all our lives where difficult things consume our days. You may have an aging parent or a child struggling in school or a health concern that feels all-consuming. Cultivating a Blissipline won't make any of those things go away. What it will do is give you hope and an occasional chuckle or reason to be grateful. It reminds you that you're not alone. And through it all, the times we value most are in sharing your bliss with other people. The best sleep happens at the end of a day spent building people up and showing up for each other.

What I Know for Sure

There are some important lessons I've accumulated since I started doing my Bliss work. I've had the chance to work with amazing men and women from all walks of life and heard their stories of failure and triumph. Significant patterns began to emerge around what fosters transformation and what keeps people stuck in the goo.

In no particular order, here are a few things I feel pretty confident about:

1. I've learned wisdom comes with age because you get really clear about what's important when you suddenly feel you have less time. Be fully present.

2. I've learned the legacy you leave has little to do with your inheritance. Your legacy is what people say about you when you're not in the room. Be honest.

3. I've learned that when you experience success in your life, there will be people close to you who won't be able to be happy for you. Be successful anyway.

4. I've learned people don't need tough love, they need deeper love, combined with good tools and a side of encouragement…hold the judgment. Be kind.

5. I've learned despite my coach training, living your best life doesn't have to involve a strategic plan or reading a self-help book a week. It comes mostly from knowing you're not broken in the first place. Everything else is just icing. Be authentic.

6. I've learned the most pressing need for the majority of people on the planet right now is just some relief from the chaos and anger. They don't need to up-level their lives so much as they just want to be able to exhale and experience some genuine peace of mind for a little while. Be able to rest.

7. I've learned a change of venue is not an escape from your thoughts. Not having access to your busy-ness amplifies whatever's rolling around in your cranium and the emotions attached to them. Leverage time away to check yourself for accuracy and purge any beliefs that endanger your happiness. Be willing to see and accept it all.

8. I've learned, at the end of the day, *your* opinion about the quality of your life is the only one that truly matters. Whether you give too much, or laugh too loud, or miss an opportunity or suffer too long. It's yours to decide if that's a problem, not anyone else. We're all on a journey of our own doing and growing at our own pace. Be YOU.

In the coming years, I will choose more often to live and let live. At one point or another, we've all made our existence more difficult than it needs to be. Ideally, lessons learned. I will focus on facilitating relief, releasing resistance and creating more bliss in the form of life simplification. I honestly think I'll take fewer vacations and create space for more peace in my own back yard.

My grandest wish for you is not quantum. In fact, it's very humble. Is it possible for you to simply know that everything you've ever hoped for is already there? Can you believe that you don't have to *earn* happiness, but just allow it? My wish for you is that you find extraordinary joy in ordinary things. It's never too late to have a happy childhood. My hope is that you never forget the truth of who you are.

I leave you with a quote from one of my favorite personal spiritual mentors…Lady Gaga,

> *"Rejoice and love yourself today. You're on the right track, Baby – and you were born this way!"*

Much Love and Bliss…

Made in the USA
Coppell, TX
17 March 2020